Being Changed in His Presence

Grace Anina McLeod

Table of Contents

1. Blessed and Highly Favored 7

2. Being Transformed In the Stillness................21

3. Maintaining an Atmosphere the Holy Spirit Can Move In 35

4. Just Call Me a Cave Dweller 51

5. Change Me Lord So I Can Fly........................65

6. Seeking Wisdom and Revelation 91

7. God's Times and Seasons............................109

8. The Fear of the Lord 125

9. Walking In Love..137

10. Building Faith 145

CHAPTER ONE

Blessed and Highly Favored

I felt the Lord prompting me to write a book. I had no idea where to begin so I started to compile a list of songs and poems the Lord had spoken to my heart over in the last year. While I was doing this, the Lord prompted me to insert different aspects of what I was going through with Him during the times I wrote them. I also began thinking about my experience in learning to hear God's voice and how to be led by His Spirit. God has prepared me for many situations that have come my way by soaking in His presence and getting revelation from Him. Many times He would speak something to my heart that I wrote in a journal. I did not always understand at the time what He was trying to say to me. But later, I would go back and compare situations I was facing with the words He had spoken to me. I would see how He knew in advance what I would be facing. It was sometimes a warning or a word of encouragement.

Later, those words really helped me go through some difficult situations knowing that my loving Father was in control. It also helped when I was not certain that I made the correct decisions in some cases. But, I could see the decisions were the plan of God. I can remember one day I felt the Lord tell me to pay off my house by the end of the year. I said, "Now Lord, You know how much I owe and how much I make. How are we going to do this?" I was single at the time. It was August. The Lord said to pay it off by the end of the year. I owed twenty thousand dollars and I only made about twenty-six thousand a year. Well, I told everyone at work if they had any extra jobs I would do them. I said, "Father, all I know to do is work extra but to pay this off is going to have to be supernatural." About three weeks later, I got a letter in the mail that a man wanted to buy my house. The man was from California and I never had my house for sale. I said, "Lord, I did not know we were moving, I thought we were just going to pay the house off." That is just one way He led me and guided me. He does not give us a five-step plan. He gives you a word and as you step out in faith, you see His plan unfold.

I have searched for fellowship with God the Father, the Son, and the Holy Spirit for the past several years. The more time I spend with Him, the more addicted I am. He showed me the truth about myself and brought me to places of repentance and surrender. I seek to be constantly transfigured into His image. For hours I will just sit in God's presence fellowshipping with Him and loving Him. I have found that being in His presence dissolved the hardness of my soul and helps me to walk in the fruit of the Spirit. I am learning I must abide in Him and then no storm, test, or trial could steal my peace. Trials had purified me and my motives so I could go behind the veil into the Holy of Holies. Walking in God's presence and seeking Him and His righteousness more than anything else has been my life and joy. Being in His presence has taught me to trust Him no matter what circumstances and no matter what situations I face. When I am in His presence, I can see Him for who He really is. I then start to become like Him.

Take us beyond the veil, to Your sweet embrace,
Take us beyond the veil where we will see Your
     face.
Take us to Your holy place, to Your holy mountain,
Fill us with Your love and grace, let us drink from
     heaven's fountain.

Your Spirit let it pour like rain over us,
Like rain let it come in waves cover us.
Like honey poured over us, let Your presence fall,
We want more of You Lord. God we want Your all.

I heard Joyce Meyer say, "That inner purity equals outer power." She said as many people as you can help, that many also you can hurt if your character is not developed before the power and anointing starts to flow in your life. So I began to ask God not to use me until I had developed the character and integrity necessary. I was seeking the fruit of the Spirit that is love, joy, peace, longsuffering, gentleness, goodness, faith, meekness, and temperance (**Galatians 5:22**). I want these operating in my life because I want to be like Jesus. The Lord would speak to me about being sanctified, being holy, being undefiled by the passions of this world, and being available to Him. I wanted what God wanted. I also wanted to be real and be around real people. I want to give God all of my life not just parts of it. I heard someone say, "He is either Lord over everything or Lord of nothing." I wanted to give Him my all. I asked the Holy Spirit to root out self in my life so I could live for Him.

> **Psalm 16: 8-11 I have set the Lord always before me: because He is at my right hand, I shall not be moved. Therefore my heart is glad, and my glory rejoiceth: my flesh also shall rest in hope. For thou wilt not leave my soul in hell; neither wilt thou suffer thine Holy One to see corruption. Thou wilt show me the path of life: in thy presence is fullness of joy: at thy right hand there are pleasures for evermore. (KJV)**

> **Isaiah 1:19 says, If ye be willing and obedient, ye shall eat the good of the land. (KJV)**

Knowing Him and knowing His voice has been my desire. I am learning that through obedience and willingness, His will is established in our lives. Through obedience we can have power with God to deliver our families, our churches, and our cities. I have found the anointing of God cost everything. You cannot get something for free. David said he would not do something for the Lord that cost him nothing **(II Samuel 24:24)**. I can remember being in church and the Lord would tell me to lay face down on the floor. I thought, "Lord, you want me to do that in front of the whole church?" The Lord told me one time in particular, "Grace, if you do not do what I tell you, you will be responsible for what does not happen here tonight." I would immediately get faced down on the floor. God was breaking pride off me. I was learning to die to what people thought and be obedient to the Spirit of God. I did not even know what God was going to do, but I did know I had heard Him. I still have no idea what those steps of obedience may have ushered in each night. I was falling so in love with the Lord. If He would have told me to do a back flip, I think I would have tried. I was learning through steps of obedience to hear His voice clearly. I would just step out when I believed I was hearing from God. I would often pray when I needed to go somewhere. "Lord, You show me where to go or what store to go to." Or whatever I was doing I would ask the Holy Spirit to help me. I was working as a police officer at the Pensacola Police Department. I felt the Lord prompt me to ask the Chief of Police if we could have prayer meeting there. The Chief said I could. I had been doing this for a while. So one day, I went to pick up snacks for our bi-weekly prayer meetings we held at the police department. I had asked the Holy Spirit to show me what store to go to. I went where I felt He wanted me to go. While at the register, I felt the Holy Spirit say to pay for the baby diapers that the lady ahead of me was purchasing. I was thinking, "Lord, I am in my police uniform." (Like the Lord did not know that). I was thinking I am representing the police department. So, I was discussing this with the Lord. The cashier ran out of tape and had to replace it. The Lord was giving me time to be obedient. The cashier got the tape replaced. She then rang up the diapers and asked the lady for the money. It was my last chance. So, I asked the lady if I could pay for her diapers because I felt the Lord told me to. She said okay and left with the diapers. I added my snacks and other items to the bill. I paid for everything and left the store. As I walked out the door of the grocery store, the lady was standing outside the store weeping. She said she had no money to pay for the diapers. She had borrowed five dollars from a neighbor but it was not enough to pay for the diapers. She told the Lord that she was going to the store in faith that He would provide what she needed. I listened to the situation she was in and prayed for her. Oh, what a glorious time that was. I was enjoying learning to hear from God. Each time I was obedient to step out He would show up. There were many other times that I did not have any confirmation that I was hearing from God, but I was stepping out anyway. The Lord was teaching me not to look at their faces or their responses. I was to just do what I felt prompted by the Holy Spirit to do. I was learning what **Isaiah 1:19** meant when it said if you are willing and obedient.

I was in training and learning to hear the voice of the Spirit of God. Once while I was volunteering my time as a police officer at a Christian music festival, Gracefest in April of 2001, the Lord spoke something to me. Someone had come to the entrance gate of the festival where I was working. They asked me how I was doing. The Lord dropped a thought into my spirit, "You are blessed and highly favored." So I said that to them, and have been saying it almost everyday since. What I did not realize was the chain of events that would follow. These events tested my faith and everything I believed in. My husband and I had dated seven years and been married thirteen years. He left me for a younger woman. I was asked to leave the church I was attending. I had all kinds of false accusations made against me at work and at the church. I did not understand what was going on. But the Lord promised to vindicate me and delivered me. I was seeking God and I said, "Lord, You said I was blessed and highly favored and look what has been happening since then." Then the Lord spoke to me about Mary, the mother of Jesus. He chose her because she was pure, holy, and undefiled. He sent and the angel Gabriel to tell her she was blessed and highly favored. The angel told her the Holy Spirit would come upon her and she would give birth to Jesus **(Luke 1:26-35).** She later became an outcast. Her friends and family talked about her, accused her falsely, criticized her and did not believe in the virgin birth. Joseph would have put her away if an angel had not come and spoken to him in a dream. Joseph was obedient and took Mary as his wife as the angel told him (**Matthew 1:20-24**).

I had been judged, criticized and misunderstood. I was called self-righteous, and so heavenly bound that I was no earthly good among other things. I thought well maybe I am reaping some of the seeds I had sown before I came to know Jesus. I would cry out to God that when people falsely accused me, God would help me to walk in love, to forgive, to defend and protect my brothers and sisters and not judge them. I so wanted to live right before God no matter what was happening around me. I knew I had to keep my mouth and my opinions off of people and their situations because I had no idea what God was doing in their lives. The Lord would tell me to anonymously send someone flowers who I knew had spread gossip that was false, or to give an offering to their ministry. I did and I believe it helped in the healing process. I found out that it is not what happens to you that is important but God looks at how you handle it afterwards. He looks at your attitude. The Word says in **I Peter 4: 8 Above all things have intense and unfailing love for one another, for love covers a multitude of sins [forgives and disregards the offenses of others]. (Amplified) Proverbs 10:12 Hatred stirs up contentions, but love covers all transgressions. (Amplified)** Love does not expose sin it covers it. I was learning everyday to walk like Jesus and to trust Him more. Those times were hurtful and difficult. I was broken before Him. We cannot go through long periods of pain with out help. Some people choose drugs, alcohol or run to other relationships. I chose to spend time with the Father. I needed help and there was no one else I wanted to run to. There were not many people I trusted at that point either. But in spending time with the Lord, my faith soared and my joy in the trials grew. I found that when you have a deep desire for the will of God in your life, there is nothing that will stop you. The more I learned about God, the more I understood that I knew nothing about what God was doing. I have become so totally dependent on Him and the Holy Spirit.

I Peter 4:12-16 Beloved, think it not strange concerning the fiery trial which is to try you, as though some strange thing happened unto you: But rejoice, inasmuch as ye are partakers of Christ's sufferings: that, when His glory shall be revealed, ye may be glad also with exceeding joy. If ye be reproached for the name of Christ, happy are ye; for the Spirit of glory and of God resteth upon you: on their part He is evil spoken of, but on your part He is glorified. But let none of you suffer as a murdered or as a thief, or as an evildoer, or as a busybody in other men's matters. Yet if any man suffer as a Christian, let him not be ashamed; but let him glorify God on this behalf. (KJV)

Philippians 1:28-29 And do not [for a moment] be frightened or intimidated in anything by your opponents and adversaries, for such [constancy and fear-

lessness] will be a clear sign (proof and seal) to them of [their impending] destruction, but [a sure token and evidence] of your deliverance and salvation, and that from God. For you have been granted [the privilege] for Christ's sake not only to believe in (adhere to, rely on, and trust in) Him, but also to suffer in His behalf. (Amplified)

"Lord, just when I thought I could not go on, not another step, like I had had enough. You under girded me and held me up. Your precious Holy Spirit strengthens me, encourages me and is the lifter of my head. What can I say except Your grace and unfailing love has kept me, carried me, and strengthened me for each battle and for each fight. I am so thankful that You reveal things to me. Forgive me when I have been ungrateful and took You for granted Lord Jesus."

I was learning to trust Him even when I did not understand what was going on. I would seek Him more and more for wisdom in every situation. I would meditate on my favorite scripture of all time, which is **Proverbs 3: 3-7 Let not mercy and truth forsake thee: bind them about thy neck; write them upon the table of thine heart: So shalt thou find favour and good understanding in the sight of God and man. Trust in the Lord with all thine heart; and lean not unto thine own understanding. In all thy ways acknowledge Him, and He shall direct** thy paths. Be not wise in thine own eyes: fear the Lord, and depart from evil. **(KJV)**

Psalm31: 19-20 Oh how great is thy goodness, which thou hast laid up for them that fear thee; which thou hast wrought for them that trust in thee before the sons of men! Thou shalt hide them in the secret of thy presence from the pride of man: thou shalt keep them secretly in a pavilion from the strife of tongues. (KJV)

I Chronicles 16:27 Glory and honour are in His presence; strength and gladness are in His place. (KJV)

I wanted to be like a leaf blown about in the wind. Blown by the Spirit of God for the destiny that He had assigned me since I was formed in my mother's womb. **The wind blows (breathes) where it wills; and though you hear its sound, yet you neither know where is comes nor where it is going. So it is with everyone who is born of the Spirit. (Amplified John 3:8)** I desired to be moldable and pliable in the hands of God. I wanted to honor Him and please Him above all else. Kathryn Kuhlman said, "I seek to get my heart into such a state that it has no will of its own about a given matter." I want that also. I would run to my secret hiding place in the Lord **(Psalm 91:1)**. I would run to His Word and His presence for comfort. In that secret place, God would encourage me. He gave me songs and poems

I believe may help others and may be for the body of Christ. One of the first songs he gave me in March of 2003 and my favorite is as follows:

Standing in His presence, what joy it brings to me
Worshipping the Master and falling on my knees.
O how I need You, I love You Lord so much
I will praise Your name forever and forever seek
 Your touch.

Oh how I adore You, I'll live with You forever
My Lord and my Savior, You are everything to me.
I thank You and I love You, I will fall on my face
To hear Your Word, oh Lord, and to feel Your soft
 embrace.

I appreciate You and all Your loving ways
I'll dance for You Jesus for the rest of my days.
Like a lamp to my feet and a light to my path
Your Word is all I need to defeat the devil's wrath.

No one else can save you but the Son of God alone
Jesus You are the Master, the redeeming Holy One.

Have faith in the Lord and in Him alone,
Stand for what you believe in for your prayers go
 before His throne.
He is faithful to answer, in His time and in His way
With God nothing is impossible, today could be
 the day.

Psalm 22:2-3 O my God, I cry in the daytime, but you answer not, and by night I am not silent or find no rest. But you are Holy, O you who dwell in the praises of Israel. (KJV)

I truly am blessed and highly favored. I know God wants to bless His people. I do not mean with just finances. He blesses us in so many different ways. And sometimes, I believe we miss out on many of the blessings of God because we do not take time to get into an attitude of worship. In the midst of everything I was going through, I would go home and put on praise and worship music and dance before the Lord. I did not know what else to do but trust Him and praise Him. When we praise God, His supernatural power will begin to manifest in our lives. The Holy Ghost moves in the atmosphere of praise. Paul and Silas prayed and praised in the midnight hour after being beaten and whipped (**Acts 16:25-26).** Sometimes we have dark times in our lives, a time of testing and trials. During those times we have the entrance of God's Word to give us light (**Psalm 119:130).** In the darkest times, we must pray and praise like Paul and Silas. Their answer came while they did. When praise and prayer come into agreement with the Word of God things happen. The Holy Spirit starts moving and doing things that accomplish the will of God on earth. **II Chronicles 20:4-12 and 20-25** are some of my favorite scriptures when battles come. It says the people prayed and the Lord said the battle is not yours but Mine. The answer and deliverance came while they were singing and praising God. I believe prayer is not effective without praise.

Let the praises begin to rise, all hail the King.
Let the earth and creation cry, let the whole world
    sing.
You cover me and sing over me, at Your throne is
    where I belong.
In Your presence and in Your courts, just You and
    me alone.

Let all the angels sing, let them dance Lord
Let them praise You and carry out Your Word.
Let them do Your bidding as You command,
Let them work over time and carry out Your plan.

God does want us to be blessed and highly favored by God and man. But we must seek Him to find out what direction He is going and learn to follow Him (**Matthew 4:19**). He will make us a channel of His blessings when we learn to be obedient to the promptings of His Holy Spirit. He wants us to step out in faith and watch Him move. I will often pray for people but God will not give me a word of knowledge or wisdom for them unless I step out. I have nothing to offer anyone. I am totally dependent on the Holy Spirit and His power. He will use an empty yielded vessel to accomplish the will of God on earth.

CHAPTER TWO

Being Transformed in the Stillness

I had to learn to get quiet. I had to quiet my mind and my thoughts. I had to learn to get my mind off my problems and myself. My soul would be troubled. I would get easily distracted. I had to learn to quiet my soul so my spirit could commune with the Spirit of God. My soul would want to think about the problems in my life, work, school, church, and everything else. I would wonder how God was going to fix different things going on in my life. My soul wanted to think about what had happened in the past. I wondered why things happened the way they did. I had to learn that my soul had to be quieted. It was in the stillness that I would get God's point of view. I had to learn to discipline myself and keep my focus on the Lord. Sometimes I would lay face down and I would start to fall asleep, so I would sit up or I would walk around. I had to be radical in keeping my focus on the Lord. But in that quiet place of total surrender, holiness is brought forth. God was doing things on the inside of me and it was beginning to show on the outside. People often want to give advice. There are so many self-help groups, magazines and books. But I learned more from being quiet than from all the voices that are in the world.

I had done so many wrong things in my life before becoming a Christian. I had smoked cigarettes and marijuana, drank alcohol, been rebellious, forni-cated, was self-centered and full of pride. I criticized and judged people without mercy. I had not been brought up in a family that knew the Lord. We knew about Him but we did not know Him. I thank God because I know He had someone out there praying and interceding for me. I would not be where I am today without someone standing in the gap for me. I was investing in all the wrong type of attitudes, behaviors and things. When I got saved, I was begin-ning to learn how to invest in eternal treasures and not what this world offers. All my life I had lived to please other people. First, it was my parents, teachers, friends, and then my husband. I would go out of my way to bless people. I wanted to be liked. I was getting my identity from being a good person, a good student and a good wife. My parents wanted me to go to college so I did. That was an honor because no one in my family had been to college. I am the youngest of thirteen children. Then I became a police officer and my identity was in that. I wanted to be the first female Sergeant at the Pensacola Police

Department because then I would have done something no one else had done yet. And I would have
a title with authority. That was not happening soon
enough, so I started going back to college and got
my Bachelors degree then my Masters degree. I then
started to work on my Doctorate degree. Everyone
thought that was so wonderful and my identity was
going to be in my educational accomplishments. I
was looking to the world to make me feel important.
I thought well if I could obtain this or do that I will be
liked or feel important. But all I had was emptiness on
the inside and I was burned out. For about six years I
worked full time, was a full time student and worked
a lot of extra duty jobs as a police officer. I thank the
Lord that I did not become the first female Sergeant.
And I did not finish my Doctorate program. I was in
my last class for my Doctorate before starting my
Dissertation, and the teacher gave me an incomplete.
His explanation was that he did not think I had the
knowledge to continue my Dissertation. I had a 3.96
grade point average. I was teaching for the university.
I had all A's and one B in this professor's class. The
President of the University stated they had no other
teacher for that class. She offered to give me another
Masters degree with Honors, because my grade point
average was so high, instead of the Doctorate. I was
shocked. I could not finish because this professor
said I did not have the knowledge but the President
wanted to give me another degree with Honors
because my average was so high. Figure that one
out. But God wanted my identity to be in Him. I was
seeking titles and praise from people and not seeking

my identity in Jesus. This was during the time I had just started getting really serious and on fire for the Lord. This was one of the many experiences I had in learning to die to the flesh. I was learning that my life is not about me. I wanted people to acknowledge me. Now, I want people to see and acknowledge Jesus. I began to ask God what He wanted from me. I would ask Him what He wanted me to do. I began to seek to please Him and not others or myself. With all my heart, I wanted to live a life of service to the Lord, putting God first.

There are many tests and trials to face in our walk with the Lord. I have found that because of the storms, earthquakes and fire, I would get in that quiet place before God to seek answers. I had to get quiet enough to hear that still small voice. In those times, I would get revelation from the voice of the Spirit of God that I needed for each situation. I did not hear an audible voice but His Spirit speaking to my spirit. The stillness came as a result of nothing-ness, brokenness, and loneliness produced by trials and hardship in my life. I would run to God's presence as an escape from the hurt and pain. In **I Kings 19:11-13** Elijah wrapped his face in his mantle. It says God was not in the storm, earthquake or fire. But once Elijah hid himself in his mantle, he could be quiet enough to hear the still small voice. I would lie on my living room floor and cry out to God to cleanse me. I would seek a closer relationship with Him because I wanted to hear His slightest whisper. I was learning to focus on Jesus. On my face, in that secret place while being still, I was learning to know

Him. I was also learning to know myself. In those silent times, the Holy Spirit would begin to stir and move. He would show me things about my life and myself that I needed to repent of and deal with. The words the Lord spoke were not always encouraging. He had to correct my attitudes, my ways of thinking and everything else about me. He was transforming me with loving correction and discipline. The people around me were beginning to see changes in me. I was starting to bear fruit from being in His presence. I would read the Word of God and begin examining my life and myself. I was learning I was not exactly lining up with what God said a disciple should be. I was willing to let God show me and change me for His glory.

II Corinthians 3:18 And all of us, as with unveiled face, [because we] continued to behold [in the Word of God] as in a mirror the glory of the Lord, are constantly being transfigured into His very own image in ever increasing splendor and from one degree of glory to another; [for this comes] from the Lord [Who is] the Spirit. (Amplified)

The Lord showed me that as a caterpillar wraps himself in a cocoon and is still for a certain period of time, that a transformation takes place. The caterpillar is transformed into a butterfly. He is able to fly, soar, and reach places he had never been before, quicker and easier. He starts to feed on the flowers and beautiful things in life and not just the leaves. He does not have to crawl anymore but can soar on the wind. I believe God wants everyone reading this book to realize where you are in this process and partner with Him to accelerate the growth. He wants us to soar without effort and to catch the wind of the Spirit. I did not understand at the time what the full impact and importance of what was being established as I met with the Lord in quietness. I was learning to hear His voice and be led by His Spirit. I believe His desire is for us to be Spirit led to accomplish His will on the earth (**Romans 8:9-7**). In those quiet times with the Lord, I would hear songs and encouraging words from the Lord. Nothing can compare to those precious times alone with Jesus. I had such peace. I was learning to hear His voice.

John 10: 27 The sheep that are My own hear and are listening to My voice; and I know them, and they follow me. (Amplified)

Isaiah 32:17 And the effect of righteousness will be peace [internal and external], and the result of righteousness will be quietness and confident trust forever. (Amplified)

Habakkuk 2:20 But the Lord is in His Holy temple; let all the earth hush and keep silence before Him. (Amplified)

As I would seek the Lord, He would encourage me and speak to my heart. I would get up each morning for several years and spend time, sometimes all day and night with my Jesus. I would take off several days at a time of my vacation and soak in His presence. I fasted, prayed and sought Him. I want to be able to usher in the presence of God wherever I go. I would cry out for an anointing that brings His presence. I wanted to smell like fragrant worship, a sweet smelling sacrifice and to have the fragrance of God on me. I learned to guard the presence of God in my life. There is power and glory in His presence. I did not want that presence to ever leave. Therefore, I could not be around certain things or people because I did not want to offend Him. I would feel the Spirit of God was grieved around certain people or conversations so I would leave. Once I had just sat down to breakfast with several police officers. They were talking about another officer not present with us. I got up to leave. They asked me where I was going. I told them I needed to get back to work. One officer looked at me and said, "Wait Grace, we have more stories to tell about other people." I just smiled. They laughed and continued their conversation as I was walking out. People would ask me, "Did you hear about so and so?" I would say I had not, and the person involved would tell me if I needed to know. I made it clear if the person who was involved in the problem needed me, I was there for them. But I would not want to get involved with gossip. I want to be a woman after God's own heart. No one can satisfy me like being in the presence of God. I never want to be separated from His presence because I love Him. But also it is where I get peace and answers to my prayers and questions. I have to ask, "What do you give your time to, your attention, your money, and your resources? What do you worship? Are you willing to pay the price for the anointing? What investments have you made for the Lord? What is your identity in?"

Exodus 45 says God is a jealous God. (KJV)

On Saturday night, I would tell the Lord, "Father, whatever time You wake me up I will go to the church and pray until the 9:00 A.M. service starts." So many times He would wake me up at 1:00 or 2:00 A.M. Sometimes I had only slept an hour or so. I would say, "Lord, I am going back to sleep and if this is really You and You wake me up right away I will go to the church." Of course, I would be awake in about fifteen to twenty minutes and drive to the church. I remember a couple of times it was raining when the Lord woke me up. I would say, "Lord, You know I do not like to drive in the rain." Immediately, the rain would stop. I would laugh and say, "Okay, I am going." The Lord was so patient with me. When I would arrive and enter the sanctuary I would immediately feel the presence of God. I did not really know the reality of His presence but I was learning rapidly. I would then go home after the 9:00 service and sleep a couple of hours. I would return to church about three or four o'clock and clean the church before the evening service. I did this for about two years. It was such a joy and pleasure to have the opportunity to serve in the house of God. The presence of God would be so awesome and so sweet. I would feel His gentleness overwhelm me. I would dance with the broom in my hand. I had the music playing and I would be so lost in the Lord by the time people started to show up for service at six-thirty.

Isaiah 30:15 For thus said the Lord God, the Holy One of Israel: In returning [to Me] and resting [in Me] you shall be saved; in quietness and in [trusting] confidence shall be your strength.

I understand there are places that you can only go with God alone. I want to go to those places. I want to be able to hear that still small voice. In those times while cleaning the church, the presence of the Lord would cover me like a blanket. I could feel Him all around me. That presence would sometimes lift as the people started to come in the sanctuary. I could not believe they could not feel the awesome presence of God. They would be laughing and talking. I knew that they did not sense the atmosphere of His Holiness. I would be grieved, as His presence would begin to lift from the sanctuary. I thought, "Lord, I come here to be with You and yet You are leaving." I did not understand and would just cry. I did not understand why they did not perceive God's presence. People may have an anointing from God on their lives but be far from God. The spiritual gifts can still operate in people that are not pleasing to the Lord.

Matthew 7:22-23 Many will say to Me on that day, Lord, Lord, have we not prophesied in Your name and driven out demons in Your name and done many mighty works in Your name? And then I will say to them openly (publicly), I never knew you; depart from Me, you who act wickedly [disregarding My commandments]. (Amplified)

I believe God will expose those people for who they really are. He will raise up the people who have laid down their lives for the gospel's sake. I see the anointing on the Godly men and women who are seeking to please God. I know that they had to pay an awesome price to walk in that anointing. They had to spend hours with the Lord in prayer and in quietness. They had to face the truth about themselves and be willing to allow God through His grace to change them. They had to fight enumerable attacks from the enemy. They had to die a thousand deaths a day to what they wanted, what they thought and what they felt. They had to fast not only food and sleep, but also things of this world.

My family played penny ante poker every since I was a child. I am the youngest of the thirteen children. We did not have much money so we played cards a lot. We continued to play after I got married. At one point, the Lord told me, "I don't want you to play poker anymore." I said, "Okay Lord." I would go to the poker games at my dad's house but I would not participate in the card game. My family criticized me at first. They were not born again at that point, and did not understand. I would just explain to them that I felt the Lord did not want me to play. It was a test of obedience. There were so many tests to come. I do not believe that my family was in sin by playing cards. But for me, it would have been sin because the Holy Spirit was convicting me not to play. The Lord would tell me I could not watch certain television shows. I had to get rid of the secular music I was listening to. Then I needed to clean out my house. There were ungodly things in my home that needed to be cleaned out. It was one thing after another. God was cleaning me up and it is a continual cleansing each day. I know that there are more tests of obedience and more areas of my life that need to be cleaned up. I am thankful that God shows us a little at a time and not all at once.

How can I describe, how can I explain,
The love I have for You I will forever proclaim.
Your goodness, Your mercy, Your love that endures
　　forever, how precious and dear.
Hold me closer. Lord draw me near.

To You Lord I give my life, it's You that I need,
How I love to watch Your hand move and see
　　Your awesome deeds.
The love and the kindness that You continue
　　to show,
Lord, come upon us and let Your Holy Spirit flow.

Engulfed in Your presence is the place I love
　　and seek,
To learn of Your humility and learn to be meek.
The fruit of the Spirit is how I desire to walk,
In action, deeds, and truth and not just talk.

I crave You. I seek You more everyday,
To know You and to be like You, it's the only way.
You fill me with joy. You have set me free,
Lord, I want to be all You have called me to be.

To prosper in my ways and follow Your Spirits lead,
An awesome and powerful life that will be indeed.
Your power and authority will set the captives free,
And open blind eyes that they may see.

**Exodus 33:12-17 Moses said to the Lord,
See, You say to me, Bring up this people,
but You have not let me know whom You
will send with me. Yet You said, I know you
by name and you have found favor in My
sight. Now therefore, if I have found favor
in Your sight, show me Your way, that
I may know You [progressively become
more deeply and intimately acquainted
with You, perceiving and recognizing and
understanding more strongly and clearly]
and that I may find favor in Your sight.
And [Lord do] consider that this nation is
Your people. And Moses said to the Lord,
If Your Presence does not go with me, do
not carry us up from here! For by what**

shall it be known that I and Your people have found favor in Your sight? Is it not in Your going with us so that we are distinguished, I and Your people, from all the other people upon the face of the earth? And the Lord said to Moses, I will do this thing also that you have asked, for you have found favor, loving kindness, and mercy in My sight and I know you personally and by name. (Amplified)

CHAPTER THREE

Maintaining an Atmosphere the Holy Spirit Can Move In

I was learning that atmosphere has a lot to do with God's presence abiding. I wanted to be sensitive to what the Holy Spirit was doing, not only at church, but also in my everyday walk. I have been a police officer with the Pensacola Police Department since 1995. It is very important in my job to be able to spiritually discern what is happening in every situation that I face on the job. I deal not only with the public, and the bad guys but also with fellow officers. I needed to learn how to maintain the atmosphere where the Holy Spirit would move. I was realizing that everything I do behind the scenes, behind closed doors, when no one is looking, effects the anointing and presence of God in my life. I was striving to live a life of holiness and purity.

I would open the church each morning before going to work. I held a prayer meeting from 4:30 A.M. until 6:30 A.M on Monday through Friday. There was a young lady who started attending the morning-prayer meetings with me. I felt the Lord tell me she would be moving in with me. He told me not to charge her anything. I was asking the Lord if He was sure that was a good idea. I just prayed about it and did not say anything to anyone. I was being selfish and did not want to give up my time alone with the Lord. My ex-husband had been gone for about eight or nine months. I was so used to having my house all to myself. I would get up in the middle of the night and dance with the Lord or pray. Well, about two or three weeks went by and one day she came to church upset. I asked her what was wrong. She said she had to be out of her room she rented by the end of the month. I told her not to worry because God told me to ask her if she wanted to live with me for a while. So, I had a roommate for about seven or eight months. I told her that a condition of her moving in was to maintain the atmosphere in my home, whether I was there or not. I did not want her watching certain television shows at my house or listening to certain types of music. I wanted my home to have an atmosphere of peace, praise and worship twenty-four hours a day, seven days a week. It was a condition of her being allowed to stay in my house. I did not tell her what to do outside my home, but in my home I had guidelines. So, the roommate agreed to live by those rules and she moved in. We learned a lot from each other about maintaining a Godly home.

We need to create and maintain an atmosphere where the Holy Spirit can move. I seek to set an atmosphere of open heavens where His presence will come and fill whatever place I am in. Where I can get answers to prayers. We need to guard and protect our hearts and the anointing to keep the oil flowing continually. We must have a pure heart and a heart focused on Him. I have found that the presence of God lifts when worldliness is present. His Holiness cannot be mixed with worldliness.

I would pour out my heart to God. I would seek Him about my life and the trials and test I had been through. I felt so much rejection once I started serving Him with everything that is in me. By the grace of God, I was trying to live Holy and to praise and worship my Lord. I was criticized for not going to movies, or watching Rated R movies that were rented by church members. I was told I was too religious and legalistic. But, I was only doing what I was led to do, or not do, by the Holy Spirit. I tried not to judge them but said I could not get by with doing whatever the Holy Spirit convicted me was wrong. I made it clear that everyone was an individual before God and I was being obedient to Him. I knew I was not responsible for what anyone else did but for my obedience, no matter what anyone thought of me. I would get up and leave the room or the dinner table if I felt the conversation was grieving the Holy Spirit. I remember when I would say what God said about me that "I was blessed and highly favored," and some church people would ask me why I could not just be real. But I thought I was being real. I had so much joy from being in His presence and no one understood that. They thought I should be devastated because of my situations. I would tell them my life is not about me, it is about Him. I would tell them if I kept my focus on Him, I could not help but be happy. But I would also seek God and ask him, "Lord is there something in me that I need to change?" I would ask the Lord if I was being real or legalistic or whatever else they told me I was. I learned to listen to what God said I was, and not people. But I wanted to search my heart. I wanted God to show me if I was being a fake, or if I had wickedness or darkness. I had times where I would lose my focus and look at my situation, but it did not take me long to learn to turn my focus back toward Him because that is where I found peace. I would never have known the peace and grace of God to the extent I do, without going through some of these trials alone. I only had the Lord to turn to. He gave me peace in the midst of the turmoil. He helped me to be about His business and trust Him with my business.

I heard Joyce Meyer say that people called her legalistic because she was living a Holy life. She said she would rather be more careful not to offend God by her lifestyle, than to do whatever she felt people were comfortable with and displease God. That is exactly how I feel. I know that through rejection God was squeezing the anointing oil out of me to bless others. The olive has to be squeezed before the olive oil is released and can be used. I felt squeezed, pulled, and crushed many times. I knew He was killing my flesh. I wanted to just pray, forgive, and keep my heart right before God in the midst of everything. I wanted to see the truth about myself. I know it takes humility, character, integrity, and walking in the fruit of the Spirit to please the Lord. I wanted that more than anything. I thank the Lord that He changes us from glory to glory. We must come to Him with a broken and contrite heart **(Psalm 51:17)**.

I come before Your presence. I'm seeking You
    alone.
To walk with me and talk with me as I bow before
    Your throne.
Coming into Your presence, gives me joy and great
    strength,
To You I owe my life. You are my everything.

I am the head and not the tail, above and not
    beneath,
Because of You my rock, my Lord, my never ending
    strength.
When I come into Your presence, Your joy fills
    my soul,
My spirit leaps and dances, as I curtsy and I bow.

I love to dance with You my King, it feels like fields
    of grace,
Where flowers bloom and life springs forth each
    and every day.
New waves of your mercy cleansing every hidden
    place,
So I can come before You and seek Your Holy face.

How precious are Your mercies, how wondrous is
    Your love,
How tender Your loving kindness, heaven's kisses
    from above.

Send Your Holy Spirit to teach me how to pray,
Teach me to love and preach. Lord, to guide me day
    by day.
I need You to lead me, to help me in all I do,
To protect me and shelter me, O Lord how I love
    You.

The shelter of Your wings, the feel of Your embrace,
You are the love of my life, my secret hiding place.
When the world would get me down, when I was
    rejected and broken,
When all had forsaken me and I felt forgotten.
There You were my King, You stood beside me. The
    lifter of my head,
You never left me. I was not forgotten. You were
    always there.

I ran to You and on Your shoulder I would lay my
    head,
As tears would stream down my face, You would
    gently stroke my hair.
My strength, my faith, my trust is in You alone,
There is no one who could take Your place, to no
    one else I'd run.

To love You and to love others, it is the greatest
    thing,
To live as Your Word says and bring glory to
    my King.
I look at the trees, flowers and the sky and I wonder
    what's in heaven, what can compare,
I see the beauty, the majesty of creation and I
    wonder what awaits us there.

I see a light shining brightly in the distance but here
    it comes,
It will overtake the darkness and many souls
    will be won.

I was crying out to God to give me more of a passion and hunger that would cause me to be on fire for Him. I cried out for throne room experiences, divine encounters and a deeper relationship with the Holy Spirit. I was seeking the anointing in every detail of my life. I want to honor God and please Him in every area. I know that will take radical obedience, the grace of God, and a lifetime. I cannot imagine where I would be if the Lord did not love me. I know He loves me exactly the way I am. He has loved me through divorce, through false accusations, through my own selfishness and pride, through lonely times, and through times when I was so crushed I felt like giving up. There were seasons in my life that were like anguish to my soul. But the Lord helped me to press through it and rise above it into new realms of His presence. I would hold my arms out to Him and ask Him to pick me up and put me on His lap.

I would need to see things from His perspective. He is my covering, my shield and buckler and He is my everlasting King. He has been there for me when no one else was. I get so lost in Him. I was falling deeper in love with Him. I found that the more I love Him, the more I hate the sin in my life and would take steps to change.

Gracious and merciful, steadfast and true.
Forever my love will burn for You.
Through the valleys and over the hills,
The love of God prevails and accomplishes His will.

Eternity is forever, but mountains will fall.
A quake will cause destruction and an end to it all.

Through the valleys and hills the Spirit of God
    flows,
To make intercession, and to help us grow.
Over rivers and streams and creeks it will go,
The plan is to cleanse us and to make us whole.

Why do we doubt and pull away?
The promises are ours if we are willing to change.
We don't have to put forth effort, just soak in His
    presence.
He will change us and transform us in just seconds.
Why don't we just trust Him and climb on His lap,
And feel His arms embrace us as He loosens the
    straps.
The things that bind us will just fall away,
To be in His presence it's where I'll stay.

Nothing can compare to the love of the King,
So gentle, so patient, He's my everything.
Nothing else matters but abiding in Him,
To praise, worship, to trust and humbly come in.
Into His presence, His throne room, His courts,
It's where I belong and it is where I find peace.
It is where I find Him and He is all that I need.

So gracious, so merciful, so faithful, so true,
How could I ever express my love for You? I love
    You Daddy God.

"Help me Lord to surrender all to You and walk
in the fullness of Jesus. Coming into Your presence
brings me such great joy. I long to be Your friend and
confidant, a loyal and trustworthy servant. I wonder
what can I give to You? A life of surrender, obedience and my love is all I can offer. Can You share
Your heart with me? Lord, am I someone You can
trust? Lord what do You prefer? What do You like?
How do I make You laugh and bring a smile to Your
face? What causes You to show up? What gets Your
attention? How can I get You to respond to me?"

I believe we can gain God's attention by walking
in love, tenderness and having unwavering trust in
Him. I remember before the divorce with my husband,
he had bought me a pair of diamond earrings. As
soon as I opened them, I knew in my spirit something
was wrong. I did not want the beautiful diamonds. I
already had one pair about the same size. Instead of
going to my prayer closet, I began to kick myself and
say, "Why are you so unthankful and ungrateful?"

But a couple of days later, my ex-husband asked me where were the first pair of earrings he bought me. I told him in the jewelry box. He said he needed them. I asked why he wanted them. He said he was going to have his ear pierced. I thought oh no, my dad will have a fit. My dad is a Marine. I then said, "Oh, I see those earrings were not really for me they were for you." My ex-husband started laughing. He walked to the bathroom. I began to cry at first, just one or two tears. I did not want him to have his ear pierced and I was hurt. Then I thought, no way devil you are not stealing my happiness or my peace over a pair of earrings. I went and got the first pair and gave them to my ex-husband. I kissed him and told him he was a good husband.

I told him to do what he felt he had to do. And I told him I loved him. I took the new pair of diamonds back to the store and returned my ex-husband's money to him. I really did not want the earrings. There were many other situations with him. The Lord was teaching me obedience and to die to the flesh. But I knew on judgment day I could tell the Lord that I was the best wife I knew how to be. I know I did a lot of things wrong but I tried to serve him and love him. I did my best to maintain the peace in our home and to love my husband unconditionally. The only way I could get through these times was to focus on the Lord and trust in Him. I would do my best to keep my mind off my situations and myself. I would praise and worship God and think about every blessing I could think of that I had. I would thank the Lord for food, clothing, shelter, and for my health.

I would thank Him for my job and for saving me. I would continue to think on anything other than my situations. I would offer the sacrifice of praise when I felt like crying. My husband was going out to bars and drinking more often than usual. He would come home from a bar drunk and he smelled like cigarette smoke. God would tell me to go show him love. I did not want to but I did. God was training me to be obedient. When I found out he was having an affair, I confronted him. He said he wanted a divorce. I did not know how I would maintain my home on the salary I had without his help. At that same time, the Lord told me to give a thousand dollar offering at church. I had never given this large of an amount before. I thought Lord I do not even know if I will be able to pay the bills. I felt the Lord impress on my heart that He would magnify Himself a thousand times in my life if I would give the offering. Well, I did not have the money so I put it on a credit card. I hated to have bills and would always pay the credit card bill in full as soon as it came in. This time I did not know how I would do it, but it was another test of faith and obedience. The Lord was stretching me in so many areas all at once. If not for the grace of God, I would have been overwhelmed. On Monday, the day after I gave the offering, I went to work. That day, I was offered eleven extra duty jobs for the month. That had never happened to me before. The amount I would be paid for working those jobs was $1,045.00. Of course, by the time the bill came in I had the money to pay it in full. Since then the Lord has told me to do other things and I asked Him to provide financially for it. I can remember another time when He told me to buy a case of thirty books. He told me specifically who to give them to. That time I got ten extra duty jobs in one day to pay for those books. I have never had one need since my ex-husband left. Not only that, I have done just about anything and everything I have wanted to do. By His grace and mercy, He sustains me. He healed every wound I had. I am not even sure how. But in the stillness of His presence, He did it. I love to worship Him for all He has done.

I know I am not in charge of my life. I must follow the unction of the Holy Spirit. I was purchased by the blood of Jesus. I am His servant. He is my Master. Through reading His Word and getting to know Him, I am learning about the anointing. I want it operating in my life. I know I must trust Him and be obedient. He wants what is best for me and He knows all. I want to see God manifest Himself in my life. I asked the Lord to break me and to go deep and cleanse me so I would be a vessel He could use. I really prayed before asking God that because I knew He would do it. I trust Him and love Him with all my heart. I want Him to have complete reign in my life. I wanted to know how I could get Him to draw near to me. I wondered how I could catch His eye and get Him to glance my way. I needed to know how to capture His heart and His attention.

Matthew 5:8 Blessed are the pure in heart: for they shall see God. (KJV)

Psalm 24 :3-4 Who shall go up into the mountain of the Lord? Or who shall stand in His Holy Place? He who has clean hands and a pure heart, who has not lifted himself up to falsehood, or to what is false, nor sworn deceitfully. (Amplified)

I Timothy 5:22 says keep yourselves pure. (Amplified)

II Timothy 2:21 says be a vessel set apart and useful for honorable and noble purposes, consecrated and profitable to the Master, fit and ready for any good work. (Amplified)

I was learning about the Holy Spirit and how He operates. I was learning to surrender to the Holy Spirit and commit myself to the things of God. I need the Holy Spirit not only in my personal life and career, but also in every area of my life every day. The Lord allows us touch eternal things if we are sensitive to His Spirit and obedient. I am so honored when He trust me to pray for His people. It is such a pleasure to serve Him and to see Him move. I would respond to calls as a police officer and knew God wanted to do something. I would ask Him why I was at that particular call. He would sometimes tell me that the person was addicted to crack cocaine and He wanted me to pray for them. The original call may have been a burglary but the person had actually traded the items supposedly stolen for drugs. There were calls where there would be a disturbance between husband and wife, but God wanted me to pray for healing of wounds between father and son. I once backed an officer on a call and the person gave their heart to the Lord. As I started to leave, the guy said, "Ma'am can I talk to you?" He stated he was about to throw himself in front of a car before the other officer had gotten out with him because he wanted to commit suicide. He said he had been thinking all day how he could end his life. He stated because he accepted Jesus, he now had something to live for. The other police officer overheard this and was overwhelmed also. God was stirring a hunger in this Christian officer for boldness and for the salvation of His people and this city. There were many calls like this. The other officers were affected because they saw how the people responded when I told them what God was showing me. Sometimes I would just be in the convenient store and pray for people. They would begin to weep because of the presence of God. I can remember several 911 calls where the person would say, "I did not call 911." One lady said she did not call 911, but asked if I could do anything about her hurting knee. I told her that I could not, but Jesus could. I then asked if I could pray for her healing. Another lady I prayed for said, "Officer, I think Jesus called 911 because He knew I needed prayer." The anointing of the Holy Spirit never ceases to amaze me. By following His promptings we can touch eternity, Glory to His Holy name! I am learning that only what is spoken with God's authority and anointing will touch men's hearts and spirits and motivate them to take steps of obedience to change their lives. Kathryn Kuhlman said, "I wonder if perhaps I had known better how to cooperate with the Holy Spirit, more might have been accomplished for God. If only I had the divine wisdom." She also made it clear that there is a great responsibility to walking in that type of anointing. That we must give God all the glory, all honor, and all the praise for each thing he does through us.

CHAPTER FOUR

Just Call Me a Cave Dweller

I would sit at home for hours and hours and I would call it my cave. I would say, "I am a cave dweller. I do not get out much." I am so addicted to Jesus. I hunger for Him and His righteousness. I know there is so much to learn. I need Godly counsel, His wisdom and knowledge from heaven. I want strategies from heaven. I tell the Lord, "I want all of you and then I want some more." I cannot seem to get enough of His presence, His touch, His warm embrace, and His soft whispers. I would cry out for Him to empty me of myself and fill me with Him. I know deliberate sin separates us from God. I do not want to forfeit what God has for me. I want God's presence and anointing and therefore, I must walk in obedience and stay in the Word of God. Some times I have felt like such a failure. I had missed God at different times. I felt I continued to fall short of God's purposes. But God is a God of forgiveness, longsuffering and a God of love. He has picked me up so many times after I have fallen. He was faithful when I was not. He blessed me and covered me even when I did something wrong. I thank the Lord that His mercies are new everyday (**Lamentations 3:22-23**). He is so good. In those quiet times, I would ask Him to teach me how I could know His ways. I wanted Him to show me how He moved and why He would move. I needed to know how to follow Him and His Spirit's lead. I would ask Him to saturate me with His presence, His knowledge and His revelation. I wanted Him to overtake me and overwhelm me.

I had heard so many people give many different methods of how to know God and get answers to prayer or whatever. I was so tired of methods because one person would say one thing and then another would contradict that and say it must be done another way. I wanted to hear directly from God. I did not want another method or formula from man. As a new Christian, I would get confused because I thought I had to read the Bible an hour everyday. I thought I had to pray for the pastors, elders, leaders, and my family. It was preached from the pulpit that the members were expected to be in the church every time the doors opened. They were to be in every service and attend every corporate prayer meetings. The members were expected to work in the church (nursery, usher, greeter, etc.). But usually you had twenty percent of the people doing one hundred percent of the work. I had to search my heart because I am a person who respects authority. I know that God sets up government and authority. I had to pray and ask the Lord what I was supposed to be doing. I wanted to pray for the people on His heart. I had my prayer list also and it is Biblical that we pray for the leaders of the church and our government. But I also believe we must be led by the Holy Spirit and not become legalistic about it. Well, I was not in every church service. I had to put my husband before church because he was not attending with me. I had to minister to him and be a Godly wife. I was attempting to show him the love of Jesus. If he was at home, I would not go to church. There were so many conditions I was expected to meet at home, at church, and at work. I had to learn balance. God was first in my life, then my husband and then the church activity. I would seek the Lord when I heard something from the pulpit because I wanted to know what God wanted and expected from me not man. I would search to know what the Word of God said about different things I heard. I wanted to serve God. And I loved serving in the church when my husband was not home. But I knew it was important that I maintained balance. After my divorce, I did the morning-prayer meetings, cleaned the church every Sunday and could really lay down my life for God. But it is important to remember not to judge others if they are not doing what you think they should be doing. We are all individuals before God and are accountable to Him. We all have different things we deal with at home and work. The Lord may want you to minister and help outside of the four walls of church. I believe the majority of my ministry is done outside of church, with people I come into contact with each day as a police officer. Many times on my nights off, the Lord would tell me to go sit across from the topless clubs and pray for the people going in and out. Or He would tell me to go walk around City Hall and pray for the leaders of the city. He would tell me to go to a specific area where someone needed ministry. I do believe we should read our Bibles, pray, and seek God. I know God wants us to come under the Godly authority in the church. But we must have balance in our lives. And we must seek God for the direction He wants us to go.

I Corinthians 1:27-29 For God selected what in the world is foolish to put the wise to shame, and what the world calls weak to put the strong to shame. And God selected what in the world is lowborn and insignificant and branded and treated with contempt, even the things that are nothing, that He might depose and bring to nothing the things that are, so that no mortal man should boast in the presence of God. (Amplified)

Teach us to walk in the paths of righteousness. Lord teach us Your ways,
Show us Your heart, train us and lead us each day.
It's Your love that molds us. Your mercy shapes us Lord,
It's Your grace that saved us. We want to love You more.

Show us Your ways, teach us Your plans, make
    straight and plain our paths,
Holy Spirit guide us to the holy places, write Your
    Word on our hearts to preach,
Spending time in Your presence Lord, until the lost
    can be reached.

O God, come down and touch Your people. Use
    Your vessels and make them gold,
Refine us Lord so You can use us, and Lord make us
    whole.
How can I touch Your heart and get Your attention?
Can we touch Your heart for this generation?
What will it take Lord? Help us to see,
Give us the wisdom and the knowledge we need.

We've cried out Lord. We've stood in the gap. Now
    what else can we do?
We need Your counsel, Your power, and might. We
    need to hear from You.
Can a nation be changed my God?

I'll declare my King to a broken generation and
    point them to the answer.
You are the solution to all things, my rock, my
    strength, Holy is Your name.

I want to know the heart of God so I can pray
effectively. I want to be able to see God and go to the
heavenlies. I wanted to learn how to develop divine
strategies and divine instructions for my family, my

church, my country, and this world. I wanted Him to show me how to take territory in the spirit realm through prayer and intercession. I wanted to know the innermost chambers of the highest heavens. I want to tear down Satan's kingdom and build God's kingdom in its place. I know that faith; relationship and intimacy with the Lord are keys to getting answered prayer. I wanted the deep things of God. I want face to face encounters with Him. God put a desire in my heart to spend those hours and days alone with Him. In the secret places with the Lord, we discover His holiness and His greatness. Through that time alone with Jesus, I could see Him in all His glory, holiness, and majesty. It makes me want to be immediately obedient in every area instantly and joyfully. Just like to caterpillar inside the cocoon. The Lord was changing me from the inside out. I asked the Lord to help me develop a mind intent on the purposes of God. I wanted Him to open the gates of my heart so I could receive from Him. I want to be the pure expression of His love when I think, act and speak.

John 10:4 The sheep follow Him because they know His voice. (Amplified)

Psalm 32:8 I will instruct You and teach You in the way You should go; I will counsel You with My eye upon You. (Amplified)

God will test us to see whether He can trust us with a closer walk with Him. He has to be able to trust us to know His secrets and His mysteries. Then we can be given greater responsibilities and privileges in His kingdom. A lot of times God will ask me questions. I have learned when God ask a question most of the time He will also give me the answer. But I really think and ponder on the questions He asks me before I give an answer to Him. I usually tell Him only He knows the answer and ask Him to show me what the answer is. While I was writing this, the Lord kept bringing me back to the things that bring a closer walk with Him. Those things are pleasing God not man, holiness, love, righteousness, and the fear of the Lord.

I Thessalonians 2:4 Says, we speak not to please men but God. (Amplified)

Hebrews 12:14 Says, strive to live in peace with everybody and pursue that consecration and holiness without which no one will see the Lord. (Amplified)

Psalm 11:7 Says, the upright shall behold His face. (Amplified)

What would you give for a night with the King?
Would you give everything?
What would you do to be part of the call of God,
And to know His heart?

What price would you pay?
Would you stay in worship?
Would you continue to pray?
Would you bow and humble yourself?
What part would you play?

Will you sacrifice all?
Will you surrender and yield?
Will you be transparent?
Can I be your shield?

What part will you play to see souls won?
What is the cost to see God's will done?
There is a cost that we must pay,
To go into God's fields, it's the only way.

I believe God has called me to intercession. Many of the things intercessors do are done in secret. We spend a lot of time in the cave or the prayer closet. Some examples of other things done in secret are fasting, giving and getting up in the middle of the night to pray. We are compassionate, merciful and gifted with discerning of spirits. We often can see the hidden motives of others. God may not always show us the whole picture of what is happening but we know when something is not right. And when we continue to pray about a situation, God will show us. We are reliable and determined about the things of God. We do not speak to soon but usually want to pray about issues until we know that we know that God has answered them. We would rather not say anything than to say God said something that we are not positive was promoted by the Spirit of God. And if we have heard from God we will not back down on what He told us. We all miss it but if the Lord speaks a direct Word, you will know it. God trust His intercessors with many personal issues about others, not to tell anyone but to pray about. God has so impressed on me that we must continually check our hearts, our motives and ourselves because God has to able to trust His intercessors. We must partner with God to pray for the needs of others. Through prayer, God can literally change a nation, a city, a family, a police department, and a church. Prayer is relationship and intimacy with the Lord.

Prayer also means listening not just coming to the Lord with request, petitions and supplication. It is communing with the Lord, fellowship, and getting to know His heart for His people. I ask Him what He wants me to pray about. The Holy Spirit alone knows what is needed for each situation. We must pray for His direction. A lot of people look at the circumstances and think God is not answering their prayers. But we cannot judge what is happening in the spirit realm by what we see in the natural realm. God hears prayer but He answers and responds to faith.

I sometimes feel the heart of God for His people and it hurts. When I see the entertainment instead of worship, the plans and agendas of man instead of sensitivity to the movement of the Spirit, it hurts my heart. I cannot imagine what God feels. I have found that prayer and pure worship are keys to heaven's storehouses. I know prayer can affect eternity and our everyday lives. I love to see God move and answer prayer. It is a joy and a great responsibility to pray for God's people. God knows we are not perfect but He chooses to use us anyway. I always say, "He uses me in spite of me." We all have some type of issues we are dealing with. He does require that we trust Him and become totally dependent on Him. Without Him we are nothing. A lot of prayer does not impress God at all. It is the attitude of the heart and our lifestyle that gets His attention. He will share His secrets with the people whose hearts and motives are pure and who are willing to spend time interceding for others. Joy Dawson's book <u>Intercession Thrilling and Fulfilling</u> says, "...Prayer is the match that lights the fuse to release the explosive power of the Holy Spirit in the affairs of men."Much of what I have shared about intercession I have learned from this book.

I was really thinking and pondering the question the Lord asked me, "What would I give for a night with the King?" He had asked me that question several times over about a six-month period. I was thinking Lord I have given everything. I had given Him control of my time, my home, my job, my money, my sleep, my attitudes, my emotions, and my eating and drinking. I did not know what else I could give. I felt I had completely laid down my life for the call of God. I had served in His house, prayed, fasted, and put Him first in every area of my life. I knew I still have a long way to go but I had tried my best to live in obedience through His grace and with His help. I was trying to learn the kingdom principles and apply them in my life. I found that learning the

ways of His kingdom are not always easy. Growth is
painful. It comes with sacrifice and dying to self.

What would you give for a glimpse of my glory?
What would you give for a night with the King?
Are you willing to lay down your life?
To give up everything?

What is the final outcome of things hoped for?
What if wishes really did come true?
What is the wish I would have for you?

What is the compensation for a job well done?
It is the love of the Father and His protection.
What would you give for a segment of time?
To come into My presence and with Me to dine?

I would give all I have both great and small,
Nothing compares to You.
Lord, I would give You my all.

When the blessings come and all is well and good,
Do not forget your first love,
This must be understood.
My plans will be established through diligence and
    hard work.
Are you willing to be that vessel?
Come let's take a look.

Let us see what the future holds,
The ups and the downs.
The price and the cost,
There is no way around.

A life of submission,
Of total surrender,
Are you willing to give that?
Oh I remember,
The promises you have made in worship and praise,
The dancing and singing in the glory for days.

You have worshipped me and poured out your heart,
Now are the days I will do My part.
The part of the covenant, you have kept and been
true,
To open your heart and do all I've asked of you.

A glimpse of the glory.
A night with the King.
What I would not give,
I would give everything.

The Lord would often put certain people on my
heart to pray and intercede for. I knew I was responsible for them before God. I would know when they
were upset and when certain issues were going on
in their lives. The Lord would give me dreams to
warn them. He would speak to me when the husband
and wife were not in unity. He would tell me when
their children were in possible danger, and all kinds
of things. Most of the time, He showed me for me

to just pray about. The person never even knew I was praying. But sometimes, I would call people on certain occasions, especially when I was at work and I knew something was wrong. Sometimes, I would be in the middle of a police call but I knew something serious was going on and it needed to be covered in prayer. I did not have time to focus and ask God what He needed me to pray about. Therefore, I would call them and ask them what the specific problem was so I could pray more effectively. I had relationship with them and they would tell me because they trusted me to pray about it and not tell anyone. There were times I did not want to say what God was showing me but I felt God wanted me to tell them. I really wanted it to be God and not Grace, so I would say, "Lord if this is something I really need to tell them let them call me." Usually within fifteen minutes the phone would ring. I would tell them what I felt God impressed on my heart but would also instruct them to take it before God. I feel it is important to always seek God on any word you get from someone because we all miss it. I used to attend church with a man named Kevin Leal. I heard him preach about using an interpreter in a foreign country. He did not like the way the interpreter was coming across with his message. Kevin is very aggressive, bold and authoritative. The interpreter had sort of feminine characteristics and a feminine voice. Kevin was very frustrated and was telling God he could not work with this man. He was telling the Lord that he needed a different interpreter. God spoke to him and said, "How do you think I feel?" I often think about that. I want to say what

God has said, nothing more and nothing less. I do not want to interpret the message unless that is the Lord's will but to just deliver the message.

CHAPTER FIVE

Change Me Lord
So I Can Fly

I would often cry out to God. I would ask Him to transform my mind, heart, soul and every fiber of my being and nature. I want to be a channel of His blessings. I want to be motivated by His voice only. I would ask Him, "Will you tell me Lord, what is the cry of Your heart? Is there anything in me that limits Your power in my life?" I did not want my experience with God to limit me. I want every limitation to be taken off. If He wants to do something new, I want to be open to it. I know God is bigger than anything I have ever experienced thus far. I would seek God and ask Him what it will take for me to walk in new levels of anointing. I had fasted certain things for a whole year and I knew it was for a new level. I felt a lot of times I was flying to low and I wanted to go higher in the Spirit. I would seek God to take all limitations and lids off me. I desired to be totally surrendered and abandoned to the Holy Spirit. I wanted to be increased and enlarged for the capacity I had for the Holy Spirit. I was learning that the closer we get to God the more our flesh must crucified. I believe it was Jill Austin of Master Potter Ministries, that said the closer you come to the fire of God, the less of you remains in the heat of His Holiness, His glory, and in His presence. The more you love Him, the more you will sacrifice to do His will. You will begin to care more about the wants and needs of others instead of your own wants and needs. Intimacy with God produces a union with His will and His purposes. But I had fasted and prayed. I had done everything I knew to do. But I still felt I was not walking in the anointing and the power of God, to the full extent of what the Word of God says I can have. I could see how I had grown but I was hungry for more. As Kathryn Kuhlman said, "I know it is not my prayers or ability but it is my surrender that moves God." We often feel we have to do something instead of just receiving the grace of God to do what He wants in His timing.

How precious and how lovely are You my ruler and
    King,
Over all the heavens and the earth, Lord Jesus
    Christ You reign.
Almighty, all-powerful, all loving, a consuming fire,
You burn away the dross so we can come up higher.
Higher into Your presence, to Your throne room we
    will ascend,

You have opened the doors of our hearts and You
   beckon us in.
With love, adoration and devotion we will approach
The Lord God our Father who takes away reproach.

I wanted to go higher but I had to go through
the process. I felt the Lord tell me to fast all kinds
of junk food (chips, cake, cookies, popcorn, everything) for a year. I was abstaining from intimate rela-
tions because, of course, I was not married. The Lord
had me fasting every Wednesday for a year for the
leadership of the church that had asked me to leave.
I thought over and over, I do not think I can make
it. God, You are trying to kill me. I felt him saying,
"Yes, that is exactly what needs to happen." I really
enjoyed reading different Christian books. The Lord
would tell me not to read anything but His Word
for six months. I was going through other rigorous
tests of obedience. I was so full of pride and haugh-
tiness. He was taking drastic measures to clean me
up. I wanted it, yet I was not enjoying the process. I
wanted the anointing that breaks every yoke but I had
to be broken first. I was being trained in obedience
to the Holy Spirit. Each day I would expect Him to
show up and do something awesome. I was learning
I would have to have ears to hear where He said to go
and do what He prompted me to do. Through impressions and promptings from the Spirit, I was learning
to know Him intimately.

Holy Spirit go with me, Holy Spirit set them free,
I want You to teach me. Holy Spirit flow
   through me,
Fill me with Your presence. I am consumed with
   You and Your holiness.

Draw near to me my Lord. With my heart I will
   praise You.
Early I will seek Your face. Thank You for
   loving me.
And for Your mercy and Your grace.

To worship You, to seek Your face,
To feel Your presence, that is what I crave.
I run to You to hide me, I run to Your salvation,
Your saving grace and Your sweet embrace.
All I need is found in You.

I would ask the Lord to reveal things, explain
them, and make them known to me. I began to see
how God takes everyday simple things and makes
them divine and eternal things. I heard Benny Hinn
say, "A divine pause can change your destiny and
through you change the world." I wanted to see desti-
nies and the world changed. I saw the miracles of
God. In my job, I have seen the Lord raise up a seven
year old child hit by an automobile who had no signs
of life. He has sent me on numerous calls where the
person told me they were about to commit suicide
and each one gave their heart to the Lord. One of the
Sergeants on the police department was healed from
a brain tumor the size of a golf ball. Cancers were

healed, detached retinas healed, all kinds of miracu-
lous things mostly through prayer, the gift of faith
and the laying on of hands. These were not everyday
happenings though, so I would cry out to God. I
wanted to see more of the promises of God fulfilled
in my life and in the lives of the people around
me. I would again go to Him and ask, "Lord what
is keeping me from operating in your blessing?" I
would search my heart. I had prayed, fasted, read the
Word, danced, worshipped and praised and sought
God's face. I did my best to keep my mind stayed
and focused on Him. I was so tired of seeing the
same prostitutes, drug user and dealers, and people
with mental problems. I saw young people dying
and I would wonder if they were saved. I wanted the
Lord to come and set people free. I would lie on the
floor and cry and feel like such a failure. I would
go to specific areas and pray for the homosexual
community. I would walk or drive around City Hall
and pray for Godly leaders. I would cry out for salvation for the city of Pensacola. I did not know if I was
doing anything wrong to keep me from walking in
new levels. I wanted to see more changes in our city.
I did not want to see the prostitute I prayed for back
out on the streets again. I wanted my prayers to be
effective. I wanted answers and I wanted more of
Him. I know in His presence people will be set free.
I have nothing to offer anyone. I was learning I am
not in control He is. People have a free will to choose
God or to choose to go to hell if they want to. But
I would read about Aimee Simple McPherson who
would enter a city and the convicting power of God

would cause people to repent and give their lives to God. I would ponder the fact that healing evangelist would empty out hospitals with the power of God and anointing on their lives. I longed to see that type of power and anointing. I love God's people and I want them free.

How do we reach a broken generation?
How do we teach them,
And show them the God of all creation?
What will it take Lord,
To change this nation?

You open doors that no man can open.
You change our hearts and heal the broken.
We look to You. We have no one else.
We need Your power. We cannot change anything
   ourselves.

Not without Your Spirit to guide us.
He leads us into all truth.
We want purity and righteousness.
But Lord look at our youth.

Look at what motivates them.
Look at what they love.
Lord, they need a touch from heaven above.

Father, please help us.
We need divine intervention.
We need the power of the Holy Spirit,
To change a perverse generation.

Help us to walk in love.
Not to judge or criticize.
But to teach them about eternity,
The importance of the prize.

The price of salvation, it has already been paid.
The cost of sin, sickness and rebellion,
Is why Our Savior came.

He did it for each one of us.
He paid the cost.
He took the stripes.
He died on the cross.

The crown of thorns were placed on His head,
The hurt, the pain, and the blood the He shed.
It was for you and it was for me.
He came, Our Savior, that we might be free.

Freed from addictions, all sin and disease.
Just look to the King, and fall on your knees.

For one day, every tongue will confess,
And every knee will bow.
But you can have freedom,
If you will accept Him now.

You can escape the fires of hell.
You can live in victory.
If you will yield yourselves to Him,
You can be set free.

You can lead a powerful life.
But it is a life of complete surrender.
To the perfect will of the Father,
Your own will, you cannot consider.

Look to the Lord of heaven,
Look to the King of Kings.
He is able to open all doors.
He is in control of all things

Lord, I cry out for the lost,
The desperate, the burdened.
That somehow you might use us,
To touch them and to heal their hurting.

Help us to lay down our lives.
Let us die to self.
Let us live our lives to help someone else.

What is the cost, Lord?
What is the price to be paid?
To see a nation and a generation changed.

The Lord would tell me, "Grace, if You seek me You will find me." I would think Lord that is all I do is seek you. I would come home after work and spend time with Him. I had a date night with Jesus every Saturday night for a couple of years. I would go to the beach or just dance with Him in the living room. Almost every day off I spent with Him. I wanted to see signs, wonders, and miracles. I wanted to change, to see the city and the people changed and to walk in the fruit of the Spirit. But mostly I wanted Him. My desire was to please Him and find out what brought Him pleasure. He is my hero you know.

Psalm 27: 13-14 I had fainted, unless I had believed to see the goodness of the Lord in the land of the living. Wait on the Lord: be of good courage, and He shall strengthen thine heart: wait, I say, on the Lord. (KJV)

I was spending so much time in His presence. I was thinking well it has been so many years. The Lord kept saying more of you needs to die to the fleshly things in your life. I would say, "Okay Lord, do whatever you need to do." But I was thinking I will be fainting any minute if I do not see some fruit and reward of my laboring. I would tell the Lord, "Father if I do not see some awesome manifestation of the power of your Holy Spirit, I do not know what I will do." He would say, "Wait, be still, die to the flesh some more and wait for My timing." I wanted to see blind eyes open, the deaf to hear and the lame to walk. I believe God put those desires in my heart because He knows my future. I believe He wants us to pray and seek the things He puts on our hearts whether for us or for others. But I also had to remember that Jesus dying on the cross is the only reason people are set free healed and delivered. There is no amount of fasting, praying, being good or doing good works that can do anything. Jesus alone is the healer, deliverer, and Master. I would talk to my friend Judy

Gliott. She would say God was speaking to her and she would give me scriptures saying wait and be still. I would say, "Judy, I do not want to hear that. I have waited for a long time already." We would just laugh. She was such a source of joy and light. I would tell her I wanted to see changes suddenly and to have a breakthrough. I would ask her if God said anything about that. We would just crack up laughing. Judy was a constant source of strength. She prayed continuously for me and for other people. I really trusted her. She is a true and lifelong friend. She had words of encouragement and would pray for me over the phone. I knew she covered me each day in prayer. I knew I could be transparent and could share anything with her. She is so faithful, merciful and humble. She hears God's voice so clearly. She would tell me, "Grace what does not kill you will make you strong in the Lord." But, I felt I needed a God encounter. I would run to my secret hiding place.

So many times every day, over and over, I would say, "I trust You Lord, in God I trust." I still do that. I confessed and read scriptures of His promises. I would feel like every ounce of anointing oil in me was being poured out to others and I had none left for myself. I had dated my ex-husband seven years and been married thirteen years. For two years after the divorce, he called me. I would attempt to minister the love of God to him. He would ask me to pray about certain things going on. I would also see him and his girlfriend because they both worked at the jail where I had to bring my prisoners. I would minister the love of God to her as much as possible. She would come and sit with me while I would do paperwork each time I brought in a prisoner. I tried to love them unconditionally and not judge them. I would pray for people all day on the job. I prayed for people at church, my friends and for the police officers. The Lord would wake me up at night to pray for different things. There were times I thought I would faint. I needed hope. So many people would call for me to minister to them and I needed hope myself. I would say, "Lord, tie me to the altar this is too hard." But God would always send me good friends to encourage me, strengthen me, correct me and speak the wisdom of God. I was desperate to walk in love. I asked the Lord to teach me about loving His people. This is what He told me:

Love is dying to self, because this life is not
    about you.
It is about forgiveness and blessing, the people who
    hurt and betray you.

There is an evil spirit behind the pain,
That comes to bring strife,
But there is nothing to gain,
It comes to steal life.

But if you return their evil with good,
That is the Father's will.
Just pray for them and love them,
And you will come up higher still.

You will have disappointments,
And you will have pain.
But in praise and worship,
I will teach you to trust again.

You can walk in love.
You can stand your ground.
No matter what comes your way,
You will not back down.

You will love. You will trust.
You will have no fear.
Because the perfect love of the Father,
It is precious and near.

It is near to those who seek Him.
He will teach us His ways.
We will be just like Him.
And have His spiritual DNA.

Hebrews 12:6 For the Lord corrects and disciplines everyone whom He loves, and He punishes, even scourges, every son whom He accepts and welcomes to His heart and cherishes. (Amplified)

God used Brad Burrus, a fellow officer and an awesome man of God, mightily in my life. He is a man of integrity. I respect him and his opinions. He always had a word that was right on with what God was dealing with me about. He would give me warnings that helped me deal with situations and even avoid some. He would tell me what I needed to hear, not necessarily what I wanted to hear. I trusted him with many situations. I would pull on the anointing of Godly wisdom placed in him. He was going through situations also, but was always an exhorter and a source of encouragement. He would make me laugh and get my mind off the situations. I do not know what I would have done without him. I thank God for good friends, who have spoken into my life, brought encouragement and covered me in prayer. It is so important to me to have people around me that hear from the Lord. I am so thankful for the anointing of God on other people's lives.

There were still times I would feel I could not take anymore. I wanted to give up hundreds of times. I believe we all have faced these times where we felt like giving up. But there is nothing in the world that satisfies like being in the perfect will of God. I know I would only be miserable if I gave up and went back to the world. I know there were times Brad felt this way and many of you may also. I could sense when Brad was discouraged and disappointed by life. Brad was on the SWAT team at the police department. He was a K-9 officer and a sniper. He worked in several different divisions of the police department. He has a lot of responsibility at work and at home. He has such a desire to preach the gospel and to help others. One day I was praying for Brad. I knew Brad was going through some hard times. I felt the Lord saying that it was between Him and Brad. I knew by the Spirit of the Lord, it was a serious time for Brad and his relationship with God. This particular day I was

working off duty and the Lord started speaking this
to me about Brad. This is what He said:

What do you do when you have done all you can?
Don't give up! On His Word you must stand.

The battle is not yours. Stand still, don't back down.
Listen for direction and it will be found.
You can hold on. You can stand.
Give it to Him. You've done all you can.

When all you have seems to fall apart,
Just know God has a plan.
He is in complete control,
Even when you do not understand.

Do not let go of Him. Seek His face.
Fall on your knees, in that secret place.

In the cleft of the rock He will hide you, just know
    that He cares.
He will always be there and He will answer your
    prayers.

He loves you and He knows your needs.
He will not leave you hopeless. He hears your pleas.
He is making you strong in Him and causing you
    to grow.
It does not always feel good and that I know.

But in Him you will find that you have great
strength,
More than you ever thought or even knew.
Yes, the problems and trials will come,
But He wants what is best for you.

They will test your love for Him. Will you let go?
They purify your heart as you continue to grow.
You are growing in Him and gaining His trust.
To know His heart this learning is a must.

Now knowing you trust Him. Can He trust you?
When it gets hard and you have done all you
could do.

**Romans 14:4 And he shall stand and be
upheld, for the Master is mighty to support
him and make him stand. (Amplified)**

**Ephesians 6:13 Therefore put on God's
complete armor, that you may be able
to resist and stand your ground on the
evil day, and having done all, to stand.
(Amplified)**

The Lord told me to give Brad this word and these
scriptures. In the job we do as police officers, we are
used to being in control. When we come to the end of
ourselves, and when we have done all we could do,
God will come in and take over. He wants us to give
Him complete control. He wants our total surrender.
One day I was telling the Lord that I felt I had been in

the valleys long enough and I wanted some mountain top experiences. I was telling Him I knew He was in control and I trusted Him. Then I told Him, "Father, I cast all my cares on You, because I know You care about me." He said, "Well that is good because I am the only one that can work things out for your good." I just laugh at some of the things the Lord tells me. It is like He was saying, "Thank goodness you are finally catching on." As an officer, our job it is to go to a situation, gain control and bring the situation to a conclusion or a peaceful end. It is not always easy to give the Lord complete control. It is difficult to hear the Lord say to wait. We want to get in the middle of the situation and fix it ourselves.

Isaiah 40:31 But they that wait upon the Lord shall renew their strength; they shall mount up with wings as eagles; they shall run, and not be weary; and they shall walk, and not faint. (KJV)

In those times when I felt I could not take anymore, I would stand on this scripture. I remember one day in particular I felt I could not take another person calling me. I had some issues I was dealing with. I was working as the Desk Sergeant and the Lord sent another officer to play me a song. I had prayed with this officer several times over the years about different issues she was going through. I know her family and she loves God. She said God told her this song was for me. The words of the song (by Luther Barnes & the Sunset Jubilaires) said, "You encouraged everyone else when you needed it for yourself and for your faithfulness it's your time." It was so encouraging and I felt my spirit man strengthened.

Well, after a couple of weeks of her playing that song for me, I did not see much of a change. Except that more people were calling me and pulling strength from me. I would spend hours with God and get strength. I would have to go to His presence to get refilled after pouring out to others. But there came a time when I did not even have time to refill in God's presence. I was working a lot. People were calling me day and night. I told the Lord, "Father, I am getting on the next boat out of here and go on a cruise if I do not have time alone with You soon." I could sense my patience wearing thin. The things I was going through were starting to bother me. I know that the only way I can walk in the fruit of the Spirit is to continually seek the Lord's face and His grace. I was getting irritated and overwhelmed because I did not have time to refill. I was asking to Lord to totally strip me of myself and clothe me in Him. I cannot image God getting overwhelmed by anything. I told the Lord I would go on a thirty-day liquid fast and asked Him to clean me up. I took communion with Him every day during the fast. I kept singing the song, "Father, make me just like You. Lord I want to be just like You. Father, make me just like You. I want to be just like You." Over and over I would sing that song for weeks during the time I was fasting.

The Lord told me,

"Look within you, Christ in you, the hope of glory."

There will come a time, there will come a day,
For My Spirit to have its way.
Over land and sea, over mountains and hills.
The love of God will flow, the earth it will fill.
My presence and nearness,
Are what you have chosen to seek and to crave,
A love that goes deep.
In My presence you will find a joy that is ever so
    sweet.

My God, my God, it is You that I adore,
I love to be in Your presence and everyday I seek
    You more.
I want to know You my Lord and walk in Your
    ways.
The nature of my Jesus is why I come each day.

I want to be more like You, molded in Your image. I
    desire nothing of myself but everything in You.
    The voice of My Father, I love and require. His
    presence I cannot describe. His goodness, the
    love, the kindness and humility, the patience and
    gentleness are what I long for, to be just like my
    Savior.

Oh God, there's nothing in my flesh that could ever
    make that happen,
But provision You have already made.

By submission to the Holy Spirit, my life He will
   change.
Ever training and ever growing, with gentleness He
   nudges me along the right path.

How thankful I am that the Spirit of God in me
   dwells,
He helps to change my heart and dig up empty wells.
Oh what love God has for His children. He is an all-
   consuming fire.
He wants the best for us but our flesh it must die.

No man shall glory in His presence and that is the
   hardest part.
For since childhood some have been taught,
If you be good and do certain things, you will earn
   the love you need.
It was not freely given; there were conditions you
   had to meet.

Now we want to earn titles, have riches and fame.
Then we will have earned the love we desire.
But what about the homeless, the nameless, the
   poor,
How do they earn the love we adore?

Though man can never meet our needs, many look
   to them,
Only to be disappointed again and again.
Hurt over and over, bitter and unforgiving,
We start to die inside and feel life is not worth
   living.

Oh the lies, the deceit the enemy will use,
To pull you away from the destiny that our Father
    would choose.
Do not be led astray,
Stand firm on the Word of God.

A legacy awaits you just around the turn.
Turn toward a loving God and the only One
    who fills.
All places that are lacking He will come and heal.

It's only His love and approval, not what man can
    give, that changes your life forever. His love is
    true and sincere; there are no hidden motives.

His love is genuine and it is true.
If you look to anyone else they will only disappoint
    you.
We are all human and we all make mistakes,
But the perfect love of the Father will forever stand.
It will fill ever purpose and fulfill every plan.

A destiny awaits you. Do not delay.
Look to your daddy God and hear what He has
    to say.

Pride must die and the flesh must go.
But He will help you along the way. You will not go
    through it alone.
Do not seek the praise of man, only the Father.
Your reputation with Him is of utmost importance.

In the heavens there is singing.
They dance and rejoice.
One day we will all be there,
If we make the right choice.

Jesus is the only way, there is no other.
I pray today people will choose to serve God only.
I pray they will choose salvation
And turn from their wicked ways,
To the heavenly Father, the Ancient of Days.

Faithful and true is the God that I serve,
He is always there for me and always keeps His
    word.
If you have heard from Him, you can write it in
    stone,
He will never forsake His Word and never leave
    you alone.

He is a constant companion.
Who can express all that God is?
He is one of a kind, mighty, majestic, holy, and
    diverse in all His ways.
He is ever changing yet always the same.
There is no explanation.
No way for me to describe the Master of all
    creation.
So vast is His wisdom and knowledge.
So awesome are His ways. He is limitless and
timeless.

The only way I can describe Him is to say He is
    LOVE. The unconditional love He has for His
    people is beyond what I can comprehend.
Forever faithful is my Jesus, until the very end.
He laughs and plays and wants to have fun.
But the cry of His heart is to see souls won.

Souls that would spend eternity in hell can learn of
    His love and freedom.
Captivity they can escape because Jesus died
    on the cross.
He took the keys to hell and set the captives free.
Open your eyes and ears and be all He has called
    you to be.

The gates of hell will not prevail against the church
    of Jesus Christ.
Victory is ours. We will not see defeat.

Give yourselves fully to the King of Kings.
Surrender your will and seek His kingdom above
    all things.
For then you will see and then you will understand,
The reason God made us, submit to His plan.

I want to see with His eyes as He sees people, and
hear with His ears. He sees us as how we can be, not
as how we are now. I want to see others through His
eyes. I want to feel His heart and learn to love His
people. I was desperate to know Him more. I asked
how I could get answers to my prayers and trust Him
especially when I did not understand. There were

dry times where He seemed so far away. I felt abandoned. He seemed distant and I would be so lonely. I would again fast, worship and go deeper into Him. My faith continued to grow because I knew His Word said He was there whether I felt Him or not. I was being stretched, molded and shaped and it did not feel good. I wonder what happens to that caterpillar when he is in that cocoon being transformed into a butterfly.

Psalm 31: 19-20 Oh how great is Your goodness, which you have laid up for them those who fear, revere and worship You, goodness which You have wrought for those who trust and take refuge in You before the sons of men! In the secret place of Your presence You hide them from the plots of men; You keep them secretly in Your pavilion from the strife of tongues. (Amplified)

I Chronicles 16: 23-29 Sing to the Lord, all the earth; show forth from day to day His salvation. Declare His glory among the nations, His marvelous works among all peoples. For great is the Lord, and greatly to be praised; He also is to be feared above all so-called gods. For all the gods of the people are idols, but the Lord made the heavens. Honor and majesty are in His presence; strength and joy are in His sanctuary. Ascribe to the Lord, you families of

**the peoples, ascribe to the Lord glory and
strength. Ascribe to the Lord the glory
due His name. Bring an offering and come
before Him; worship the Lord in the beauty
of holiness and in holy array. (Amplified)**

I attempted to center all my focus and attention
on my Master. I pondered my life because I wanted
to please Him in every area. I would judge myself
and search my heart. I wanted to be pure, holy, and
have clean hands. I am so delighted with Him and
devoted to Him. I wanted my life to be a sweet
smelling sacrifice. In His presence is fullness of joy
(Psalm 16:11). I wanted closeness and intimacy with
my Savior. I was learning to trust Him in the midst of
all the uncertainty life brings. The Lord was teaching
me the many ways of His Spirit. I was learning
how to interpret the right flow, the right direction
and how to go the right way. I heard Pastor Keith
Moore teach on being rein trained. This is where a
horse does not need a bit in his mouth to force him
to go the right way. The rider just lays the rein on the
right or left side of the neck. Because of the horses'
obedience, he goes whatever direction the rein is laid
on. I said, "Lord, I want to be rein trained by Your
Holy Spirit." I asked the Lord to show me how to
administrate the anointing. I sought to have a deep
respect for the Lord and for the Holy Spirit. I could
see that as I obey God, He becomes more real to me
and manifest Himself more. He reveals Himself as I
obey and respond to His promptings. He wants us to
walk by faith and trust Him. He does not always give

specific instructions, just vague words, impressions, or promptings so we will trust and walk by faith. He wants us out of our comfort zones and focusing and relying on Him. I have so much to learn. I do not want to miss anything God has for me.

Who loves you O Jerusalem? Who needs you saints of God? Who walks on crystal waters? Who paints the skies above? Who comes first with a warning?

Do you hear My calling to you? Go over here. Go this way.
Do you hear My cry? Come to me, come to Me My child.

Do you hear My cry? Do you hear Me? I call to you, do My will.
Do not go astray, no that is the wrong way. Do you hear Me calling to you?

Consume me with Your will my Lord. Let me hear Your cry. Let me hear Your voice my God. Your voice I will listen to, Your voice I will hear. It is You I seek. I want to do Your will.

Let me hear You, let me see You, You are my source, speak to me. I am crazy for You.
Open windows of heaven for me to see, help me focus on You, to sense Your presence, to know You.

Do you hear Me call? Do you hear Me sing over you? Do you know My love? Do you hear Me call?

Help me find what is in me, help me to hear Your heart, help me to be real. I want Your will and to please Your heart.

CHAPTER SIX

Seeking Wisdom and Revelation

I would seek God's wisdom and revelation. I would study, make sermons and have preached some of them. I was learning from the Holy Spirit by what I heard on tapes, heard preached, read in books, and read in the Word. I was learning that atmosphere has everything to do with revelation. There is a song I love to sing (You are Holy-Hillsong Music The Platinum Collection Volum 2). It talks about the holiness of God. It says, "I'll sing Your praises forever. I'm deeper in love with You. Here in Your courts where I'm close to Your throne. I found where I belong." In the atmosphere of worship, we become transparent before God and have intimacy. I find the closer I get to Him, the more I find myself repenting. I have found that if I compare myself to people in the world and even some other Christians I do not look that bad. But when I compare myself to Jesus, I see what a sinner I really am. The only thing that matters is if we look like Him. After repenting, I would just praise Him, thank Him, and worship Him. Tommy Tenney, I believe said, "Praise splits open the heavens but worship invites in the King." As we worship, the Lord gives us eyes to see in the spirit realm. I would worship the Lord and the glory of God would fill my home. Sometimes I could not even stand. I would lie on the floor and weep. Around that same time, I was opening the church for prayer each morning. I would just love on the Lord. I danced, worshipped, and listened. I would pray if He put something on my heart to pray about. But mostly I just wanted to be with Him. I wanted to learn of Him and know Him. I continued to do that unless God prompted me differently during the morning time. The time I spent with Him in the morning was a special time set apart to just be with Him. The glory of God would fill the sanctuary on some mornings. I wanted to refuse to go to work. I did not want to leave the atmosphere of His glory and His presence. To a certain extent, His presence went with me but I had to concentrate on my job. When I took my focus off of Him, His presence was not as intense. In His presence I was learning and growing in wisdom and revelation.

Amos 3:7 Surely the Lord God will do nothing without revealing His secret to His servants the prophets. (Amplified)

I heard Kevin Leal preach that you do not break the laws of the kingdom. The laws of the kingdom break you. They break the spirit of pride, rebellion, unforgiveness, bitterness, etc. How true and wonderful that is. I want my life to line up with God's purposes for me. I love His statutes and commandments **(Psalm 119)**. God gave us the law for our good. It helps us to be free. I needed to understand and know what God wanted to do. I want to carry the Lord's secrets. I want to live in the Spirit. In intimate times with Him we learn. When we take time to be in His presence, we get to know Him, His ways, His heart, and His character. Through tests, trials and temptation our inner man is strengthened and our character is established. Those tests and trials bring us to our knees and keep us at the feet of Jesus. God is calling us to receive the knowledge that only comes through experiences while we have been at His feet. We must come before the Lord with an attitude of reverence, humility, brokenness, and submission. The more we grow in the knowledge of Him, the more the Spirit of wisdom and revelation will increase in our lives. The combination of revelation from the Holy Spirit, faith, and obedience are what brought the power that Jesus walked in. Some of the many aspects of God's nature are in **Isaiah 11:2.**

Isaiah 11:2 And the of the Spirit of the Lord shall rest upon Him- the Spirit of wisdom and understanding, the Spirit of counsel and might, the Spirit of knowledge

and of the reverential and obedient fear of the Lord. (Amplified)

Ephesians 1: 17-19 That the God of our Lord Jesus Christ, the Father of glory, may give unto you the spirit of wisdom and revelation in the knowledge of Him: The eyes of your understanding being enlightened; that ye may know what is the hope of His calling, and what the riches of the glory of His inheritance in the saints, and what is the exceeding greatness of His power to us-ward who believe, according to the working of His mighty power. (KJV)

I would meditate and read aloud this scripture everyday for several years. I definitely and desperately need to have an increase of the spirit of wisdom and revelation.

2 Peter 1:2-4 Grace and peace be multiplied to you in the knowledge of God and of Jesus our Lord, as His divine power has given to us all things that pertain to life and godliness, through the knowledge of Him who called us by glory (honor, praise, distinction) and virtue (moral excellence/righteousness), by which have been given to us exceedingly great and precious promises, that through these you may be partakers of the divine nature, having

escaped the corruption that is in the world through lust. (KJV)

I was reading a teaching emailed to me from Todd Bentley's ministry and it gave several things that stir up the gift of wisdom and revelation. The first thing he said about revelation is that it is always connected to the intimate knowledge of God. **II Peter 1:3** says God has given us His divine power for everything pertaining to life, and to activating the provision of everything we need to live a life of godliness. It is all connected to the intimate knowledge of Him, through prayer, intimacy, worship, sitting at His feet and being in His presence. The divine nature, character, spirit and personality of Christ Jesus are imparted to us in intimacy through revelation. That impartation and transformation comes as we are in His presence. Just like the caterpillar is transformed while in the cocoon, we can be transformed while in His presence.

I need God like food and water. I cannot live without Him. I love His presence. It is not about just wanting to spend time with Him. I need Him. I need the wisdom that comes from knowing Him. One day several officers were attempting to serve an arrest warrant on a suspect at an apartment complex. The suspect jumped out of the balcony of a second story apartment building and hit the ground running. The officers gave a description of the suspect and what he was wearing. I responded with other officers. I parked and asked the Lord where to go. (I love chasing the bad guys but more than that, I love catching them). After a few minutes, I felt the Lord told me to go down a certain street and I did. I saw the suspect running down the middle of the street. He had changed pants and was wearing a different color over his other pair. But I knew this guy was the suspect we were looking for. I had never done this before, but I felt led to do it so I did. I pulled up next to him in my police cruiser. I rolled down my window. I said, "Are you tired of running?" He stopped and so did I. Still in my cruiser, I said, "Why don't you put your hands on my car?" He complied. I got out of my police car. I said, "Put your hands behind your back." He did and I placed him under arrest. The Lord gave me wisdom in so many situations on the job. Like I said, I need him. Over and over the Lord has helped me. The other police officers would say, "Grace, you were not out of breath on the radio, what happened?" I would tell them what God did. I would not have to chase anyone. They were subject to the authority of God. One of them said, "You do not need us to back you up. You have back up already." I assured them I did need them also.

Bentley said meditation is one thing that stirs up wisdom and revelation. **2 Peter 1:4,** teaches us about the exceeding great and precious promises of God. Confessing scripture, praying it, reading it, thinking about it, meditating on it day and night, His Word becomes a lamp to our feet and a light to our path. This is how we experience the exceeding greatness of His precious promises. Bentley said in the email that meditation brings revelation and revelation brings manifestation of what has been revealed. This is one thing I have dealt with. Once God revealed something to me, I would think there would be immediate manifestation and sometimes it was years before I saw the manifestation. I had to learn to keep His Word ever before me, to meditate in the Word of God day and night. After I got the knowledge from my head to my heart, I would see the manifestation. I would quote out loud and meditate on certain scriptures every day for years. I did this even before I understood about the power of the Holy Spirit and the direction He would give if I depended on Him. I was brought up in a Catholic Church. It had programs that were written years in advance. During that time, the church did not allow anyone to bring a Bible to church. The church had a book you would follow each service. You never depended on the Holy Spirit. I did not even understand at all about the Holy Spirit. But He knew me. He prompted me to read those scriptures. Sometimes in that Catholic Church, the Holy Spirit would come upon me and I would just weep. I never knew it was the Holy Spirit until later. I did not know why I was crying. Sometime in 1997, I believe, I started really getting serious about serving God. I was prompted to start listening to Joyce Meyer. I was a baby Christian and needed to grow. I listened to her everyday. I bought over fifty of her teaching albums. I still listen to them over and over. I got rooted and grounded in the Word through her ministry. I saw myself transformed as I put to practice the things she taught. I got a deep foundation in Jesus and the Word. Even though I was learning, I still did not know much about the application aspect of the supernatural. I was learning to hear God's voice as I did what Joyce taught. But I still did not fully understand it. I was also learning about God, His nature and character.

Bentley shared in his teaching, that Godly character is a key to stirring up wisdom and revelation. **2 Peter 1:5-9** We cannot become like Jesus and what He wants us to be without being in His presence. Godly character continues to grow as we yield and submit ourselves to the Holy Spirit's cleansing process and as we submit to the discipline of the Father. I heard a pastor say, "You cannot be in the beauty of His holiness and not deal with the sin issues in your life." We are barren and unfruitful in the revelation in our lives because of our character or because we are not full of His Word. If you have not been meditating on God's Word day and night, you cannot have revelation. We must do everything according to the Word of God. As we meditate on the Word of God and live in intimacy with the Lord, we will share in His exceeding great and precious promises. We will develop the qualities of His divine nature and character. I have a passion to be Christ-like. Going beyond the veil, we encounter the grace of God and we are changed. My goal is to be like Jesus. I want to be transformed in His image, to look like Him, to act like Him, and to love like Him. I do not want to just work for God. I want relationship with Him. I worship the Master because our reward is to know Him. He is our reward. God is the major source of meaning and fulfillment in my life. I ask Jesus to help me seek His face. I ask the Holy Spirit to take me to a higher place in the spirit realm. I was made to worship Jesus. I ask the Holy Spirit show me how to worship in spirit and in truth and show me what to do. I have found that man looks for gifts and talents and often promotes based on this. But God promotes based on character and integrity, not talent and ability. Through constant crucifixion of the flesh and being moldable and pliable in the hands of God, we develop Godly character. I wait in God's presence expecting to hear from Him. I sit down with a pen and paper. I write the date on the page and just wait on God. He may show me something or He speaks to my spirit, but I just wait. Jesus often withdrew into the wilderness or the mountains and prayed. He spent time alone with God. I believe He was refilling after giving out all day. I believe He was also praying and interceding for the people. In Bentley's article, another key to stirring up revelation and wisdom is waiting for God's counsel.

Psalm 106:13-15 But they hastily forgot His works; they did not wait for His plans regarding them. But lusted exceedingly in the wilderness and tempted and tried to restrain God in the desert. And He gave them their requests, but sent leanness into their souls and disease and death. (Amlpified)

O Lord my God, You are amazing, I will never go
    away,
You are the light of my life. I will never go astray.
O Lord my God, You are amazing. You are my life.

You are the very air I breathe. You are so good
    to me.

O God of wonders You are unsearchable,
Early will I seek You, You take my breath away,
I love to dream of You. I think of You all day.
I ponder the works of Your hands, the beauty
    of it all.

Each day I rise and seek Your face,
I seek Your mercy and Your grace,
What is the total sum of Your love for me?

O Lord I love You with all that is in me,
Lord I need You. Please walk with me,
In the cool of the day I find You near to me.
Each morning and night I seek You. Lord, come
    close to me.
You are the one I love. I delight in You,
You are the truth and light and there is no one else
    like You.
Who can compare to Your matchless love?
Who can express? Who sent His only Son?

What love I have for You,
My desire is so strong,
What hunger and thirst I have for You alone.
You are my rock, my redeemer, my unfailing King,
My husband, my Master and Lord of all things.

You control the world. It is all in Your hands.
I look at creation and try to comprehend,

O God of wonders, You amaze me,
I stand in awe of You as I look at what You do.
How can I express my love for You?

I love to sing You songs, write to You and try to
    express my love,
But I cannot seem to put in words all that I feel.
My love is stronger than an ox.
My heart burns for more of You.
I cry out in desperation Lord because I want You.

Manifest Yourself to me,
Let me know Your heart,
Teach me Your ways my Lord,
I want to do my part.

I want to see Your glory,
Your goodness I will proclaim.
Forever I will love You,
And sing to You my King.

I will pour out my heart,
In love songs to You O Lord,
There is no one like You.
It is You I ADORE.

Like sweet smelling perfume, like a wonderful
    fragrance,
That is what I want my life to be, to ascend to Your
    throne.
The fragrance of worship, my life I will bring,
A fragrant odor before my King.

Lord cleanse me, purge me, purify my heart, so I
    can live a life pleasing to You.
I desire pure motives, pure thoughts and deeds that
    bring You joy.

If You would only help, I cannot do it alone.
I want to be pure and come before Your throne.
To wash Your feet and live a humble life,
To be broken and contrite,
To walk in love and forgiveness is what I want.
To be like You Jesus is what I strive for.
Help me Lord, help, me be pure.

A holy life, a sacrifice, a bow before the King,
On my knees sometimes at night, to You my Lord I
    sing.
I will dance day and night with a thankful heart,
For all You do and who You are, Lord where
    do I start.

Where can I finish and what can I write?
All that You do is so marvelous it would take a life-
    time to tell,
The love and gratitude I feel and how You have
    become so real.
In this cave I live, it is my secret hiding place,
It is where I seek You Lord. No one can take
    Your place.

I seek You. I need You. The world has nothing
    I want.
To be alone with You seems selfish.
But nothing can compare to the time I spend
    with You.
You I call, You I seek, it is You I want to come,
Father I cannot help it. I want You alone.

I want God's fragrance on me as I soak in His presence, in the glory of God. We develop intimacy with
Him when we come to Him for who He is, not for what
He can do for us. I ask the Lord to take down every
veil in our lives so that we may see Him and get the
wisdom and the revelation we need. Whose glory are
you seeking? What do you spend your time doing? If
the Pastor calls a prayer meeting do you show up? What
about if the Pastor says he needs someone to clean the
church? But if I told everyone reading this, I will give
you $100 each if you show up at your local church at
0300, a bunch of people would be there. They would
tell their friends and they would be there too. Whose
glory are you seeking? Where are you getting your
glory? Do you seek titles? Why do you do the things
you do? Do you need a pat on the back? Do you tell
everyone? I used to do a lot for people but I would tell
everything I did. People would tell me how wonderful
I was. So I believe I got my reward. I wonder when I
get to heaven will there be any good works that I did
without telling anyone. I want to be appreciated by
God. But it is so hard not to try to take some of the
credit man gives. Jesus would tell people He healed not
to tell anyone. He was not seeking His own glory. I ask

the Lord to let everything I do be for His glory, to build His kingdom. I try to make decisions based on what is best for His kingdom. I try clean the church as if God asked me to do it and I get my appreciation from Him. I do not want to do what I do for the honor of man but for the honor and glory of God. But we do seek to be appreciated by man unless God changes us. We have got to seek wisdom in these areas.

Proverbs 2:1-5 My son, if you receive My Words and treasure My commandments within you, making your ears attentive to skillful and godly wisdom and inclining and directing your heart and mind to understanding; yes if you cry out for insight and raise your voice for understanding, if you seek [wisdom] as for silver and search for skillful and godly wisdom as for hidden treasures, then you will understand the reverent and worshipful fear of the Lord and find the knowledge of God. (Amplified)

As I come before You Jesus,
And I look to You alone.
Your joy fills my heart,
And I want You for my own.

Coming into Your throne room,
It is my secret hiding place.
It is where I share my life with You,
And it is where I behold Your face.

I soon forget myself,
And I am consumed with Him.
Joy floods my soul,
And I see many gems.

Like a diamond as you turn it,
It sparkles and it shines.
It catches your attention,
And you study it for a time.

I study You my Lord. I look to You.
And I see something new each day.
You are so beautiful and unique,
Show me more Lord. Do not delay.

My hunger starts to burn,
My passion continues to grow.
I forget the rest of the world,
For it is You I long to know.

I seek to usher in Your presence everywhere I go.
Then lives will be changed and people set free,
It will be glorious You know.

The city will be a different place.
As the Shekinah glory fills every space.
The darkness it will have to flee.
As God comes in power and authority.

There will be signs, wonders, and miracles,
They will be to numerous to count.
We will give God all the glory,
We will let out a triumphant shout.

Let every hospital be emptied.
Let all the sick be healed.
Let all the nations view it,
And to the Lord Jesus let them yield.

How marvelous are Your mercies.
How wondrous are Your ways.
How beautiful Your white garments.
Let us lift our hands in praise.

Again I see the gems,
Sparkling and shining like the sun.
Reminding me to the nations we must go,
And the souls that must be won.

It is all for You Jesus,
My hero, My Lord, My King.
My Master, My Provider,
In all the earth You reign.

You reign in my life and in my heart.
It is only You I aim to please.
Lord God I want to do my part,
So, I will stay on my knees.

I believe God has put greatness in all of us. It is to touch the world for His glory. I pray and ask the Lord to pull that greatness out of us to build His kingdom. I want to do great things for Him. I believe that even our prayers are inspired and lead by the Lord. He gives us the desires we have and prompts us to pray for those things He has put into our hearts. I like to believe that most everything I do is lead by the Spirit of God. I see how He orchestrates meetings and divine happenings that only He could have done. Even when I watch different Christian shows or read a Christian book, He will speak to me through them. I attempt each morning to yield myself to the Spirit of the Lord. I need His wisdom and guidance each day. All these poems and songs sound real good because God put them in my heart. But in reality, I am not living with the Lord totally reigning in every area of my life. Everything I do is not for Him yet, there is still a lot of Grace McLeod that needs to die.

CHAPTER SEVEN

God's Times and Seasons

I would also study God's times and seasons. I felt
some times I had failed in the things I would try
to do. And actually, I did fail a lot. I missed God. I
had to learn. The only way to learn is through stepping out, making mistakes, and learning from them. I
felt God say, "These times of difficulty that we walk
through are not failures but seasons of training and
preparation." God shakes things up in our lives, pulls
us out of our comfort zones and then realigns and
restructures things according to His will. We may not
always like it but when God says move, we have got
to move or we will miss out on what God is doing and
accomplishing. We cannot control times and seasons
only God can. I can remember only a year or so after
my divorce and there were no hugs or kisses from
my spouse, I would get lonely. I would say, "Okay
Jesus I need you to come on down here and show me
where my future husband is." (I got that saying from

my friend Judy, "Okay Jesus I need you to come on down here"). But no matter how lonely I was, I knew I wanted God's timing and His chosen man for my life. I would just attempt to cooperate with Him and be faithful to Him. I would continue saying, "I trust you Lord. In God I trust." The Lord told me, "In My time and according to My will things will be established, accomplished and released in your life."

Someone told me I needed to write down the things I wanted in a husband because Jesus was going to bring my husband soon. So, I wrote about three pages. I covered everything I could think of. I had so much fun. I laughed and laughed as I read the letter. I thought, "Lord if there is a man out there like this and he is not already married it will be a miracle." God is in the miracle working business you know. I showed the letter to a lady who is usually a critical person. She said, "You want Jesus, this man is perfect." I laughed and laughed again. I told her she was right and I would not settle for anything less. She said, "You need to add some exceptions of what you would settle for if he does not meet these standards." I told her if he did not meet the standards, he was not the man God had for me. The list contained mostly Godly characteristics, integrity, and submission to the Lord. I love the Lord with all my heart and if it was His will that I never remarry, I would accept it and love Him. His will is all that really matters. I did later receive that wonderful man of God but he was God's choice for me. I did have to settle for not perfect yet, but knowing God was perfecting us both together.

I was learning through this process of training and preparation to get ready for the fullness of God's plan and not try to rush anything. One day I would ask for something, then I would say, "Lord, I am happy where I am with what I have. My times are in Your hands." I was learning that when God knew I was ready He would bless me. I would attempt to magnify God no matter what was going in my life. I would talk about the problem solver, my Jesus and the only solution, instead of the problem. I have found that as we go to new levels with God, we need more insight and understanding. We have to be so sensitive to the Holy Spirit leading and guiding us to make the right decisions.

I was working as a School Resource Officer in one of the schools in the city. All the schools were having bomb threats. The school I was at had thirteen in about a month's time. My Sergeant (a man of God) and I got together. I said Sergeant we are going to have to take authority over this in the spirit realm. He said, "Okay what do you want to do." I said let's meet at the school and pray. We called several other Christian officers and prayed for two hours at the school. We looked up scriptures about bringing people to justice for wrongdoing and read them out loud. The Sergeant felt we should also fast for twenty-four hours. We all agreed. We prayed that not only would the bomb threats stop but that the people responsible would be prosecuted. Within a very short time, I had made several arrests. We only had one other bomb threat that year and it was around six in the evening when no children were at the school. The other schools continued to have the threats all year and sometimes three or four a day. I told each school administrator and School Resource Officer, what we had done but they refused to do it. The media wanted a press release on how we stopped the bomb threats at our school. I told our media personnel at the police department that we fasted, prayed and sought God. She said the local paper would not print that. I told her, "Well that is what happened." I also explained how the perpetrators were caught. They only printed partial truth giving myself and another officer the credit for doing a good criminal investigation. It was only by God's goodness and grace that we had evidence enough to catch the perpetrators.

I feel I have somewhat entered into the promise land. I have just put my feet on the land, and I am walking in it. I have been reading Joshua and when God brought them to the promise land they had two setbacks. In Joshua 7, at Ai Achan took some of the devoted things that God commanded them not to do. And Joshua made a covenant with the Gibeonites. I do not want setbacks. I desire to walk and work with God, to cooperate with Him in the good times and bad times. I have felt so isolated and hidden as God has set me aside to train me. He had to remove all things that were distracting me. I am so thankful for all He has done. I read how God separated Moses, Joseph, David and others in the Bible. I know it is part of the process to fulfill His plans. I would have never known the grace and peace of God to the extent I do if I had not gone through some of these things. I know the Lord has been training me for leadership and that it is a lonely position. I choose to separate myself from the world and be holy in order to carry the anointing of God on my life. God has been equipping me through the test and trials for my call and my destiny. God must adequately prepare us for our assignment to see us succeed. I trust Him so completely. He continues to stretch my faith. My trust is ever growing in Him.

Romans 1:17 For therein is the righteousness of God revealed from faith to faith: as it is written, The just shall live by faith. (KJV)

Joshua 1:7-8 Only be strong and very courageous, that you may do according to all the law which Moses My servant commanded you. Turn not from it to the right hand or to the left that you may prosper wherever you go. This Book of the Law shall not depart out of your mouth, but you shall meditate in it day and night, that you may observe and do according to all that is written in it. For then you will make your way prosperous and then you shall deal wisely and have good success. (Amplified)

I am not even sure to the full extent what God has planned for me and I do not need to know. I take life one day at a time. We are not even guaranteed tomorrow. I want to do what God has called me to do on that particular day. I am learning to trust Him completely. The Lord would tell me at different times, not to forget where I came from and what got me to where I was. He would remind me to continue to fast, pray, read His Word and be good to others. I seek to follow the Lord carefully and wait on Him. Sometimes the fight to stay on course and do the right thing is intense, but when God births His plan, it will all be worth it. I know once I learn to fully surrender and completely submit to the perfect will of God, the destiny He has for me will come to fullness. I will then walk in the anointing and presence of God like never before. I want to know Him and what attracts Him because I have nothing to offer anyone. It is His presence that changes us.

Sometimes God comes suddenly and shifts our lives in unexpected ways. I have experienced this several times. I have found this to be true in my job, in my family, and in my church. When walking in these new paths and new ways we must be obedient to God and hold fast to His promises. On one such occasion, I was asked to leave the church I was in. It was because the Lord had me confront an issue. I wanted to run from it but the Lord told me I would be responsible if I did not confront the sin. People I thought were my friends had betrayed me. False accusations were made. I did not know whom I could or could not trust. There was a shift about to take place. I knew nothing about it and I was not ready for it. I guess I always want to think the best. I knew I was being obedient to the Lord. I was not judging others but said I would under gird them in prayer.

I was still expecting them to walk in love. After confronting the person and nothing changing, I told some of the elders the situation I was in. I brought witnesses like the Word says if the person will not repent. They asked me to come to a meeting. Before the meeting the Lord asked me these questions.

My beloved so true,
Will you do what I ask of you?
Will you stand firm and hold your ground?
Will you walk straight and not back down?

I will strengthen you.
I will give you peace.
I will equip you with all that you need.

Just ask what you will and it will be done.
Lord, the cry of my heart is to see souls won.
You have put a desire in my heart to see people
    set free,
From bondages and sickness and all kinds of
    disease.

I was submitted to the leadership of the church where I was asked to leave. I had never been a problem at the church. I had never had any type of counseling or discipline. Even through my divorce, I trusted the Lord. I never received any counseling from the leadership. I advised the leadership of the church what was going on with my ex-husband but they never offered counseling. I did not think to ask for it for myself and my ex-husband had already told me he would not go. I had keys to the building and spent a minimum of twenty to twenty-five hours a week in the sanctuary praying for about two years after my separation with my husband. I would go to church with a single focus and that was to get in God's presence. I did not have a lot of real close relationship there except with about six or seven people. I was very rooted and grounded in the Lord. But this incident with the church almost shook my faith to the point I wanted to give up on God.

I have only a few times in my life gotten a "Thus sayeth the Lord" word. Just before the meeting, the Lord woke me up in the middle of the night. He said, "Thus sayeth the Lord, A bull dozer anointing is about to come upon you. You will plow the fields of unbelief. You will plow the fields of corruption. Nothing will be left uncovered but will be overturned. It will wreak havoc on injustice." I had laid down my life for the Lord, but I felt that also included this church and the people in it. I had no idea how God was going to come with a suddenly and shift me out of my comfort zone. Now as I look back, I see how God did prepare me. I looked at the different things He spoke to my heart that I had written down the six months prior to the meeting where the leaders asked me to leave. Some people came later and admitted to me what they did wrong and asked for forgiveness but most did not. The Lord told me exactly three months before the meeting, "Your reputation with me is untarnished. Your reputation with others, you will loose to fulfill all I have for you. I am your vindicator." I was so thankful that I knew that what

I did was of God and not Grace. They had asked me to leave the church. I felt a bit beat up by this experience at first. On the way home one of the elders I had trusted, but that had actually turned his back on God that day, called me. He asked me how I felt. I said kind of beat up like I had a black eye and bloody nose. I then said, "But if that is all you guys have, you need to go get some friends." I felt like I could run through a troop and leap over a wall **(Psalm 18:29)**. I felt I could conquer the world if I was obedient to do what the Lord said and not back down. I knew I had stood up for what was right, but mostly I stood up for the Lord. It was after this, that the Lord gave me most of the songs and poems in this book. I was learning to love when others did not, sing when I felt like crying, laugh when I felt blue, praising God when I felt like quitting, and believing when it looked like all hope was gone. I had faith when I saw nothing was going my way. I was trusting God for the times and seasons of release. I believed in God's goodness and mercy that is unfailing. The Lord told me, "All things will come in due time. I am never late but right on time." The Lord wants us to be a living sacrifice. He expects us to die to ourselves, what we want, think, and feel. The Spirit of God must lead us for our lives to be effective.

Romans 12:1 I appeal to you therefore, brethren, and beg of you in view of all the mercies of God, to make a decisive dedication of your bodies as a living sacrifice, holy and well pleasing to God, which

is your reasonable service and spiritual worship. (Amplified)

Romans 8: 12-14 So then, brethren, we are debtors, but not to the flesh, to live of the flesh. For if you live according to the flesh, you will surely die. But if through the power of the [Holy] Spirit you are putting to death the deeds prompted by the body, you shall live forever. For all who are led by the Spirit of God are sons of God. (Amplified)

I Peter 3:4 But let it be the inward adorning and beauty of the hidden person of the heart, with the incorruptible and unfading charm of a gentle and peaceful spirit, which is very precious in the sight of God. (Amplified)

Hebrews 1:9 You have loved righteous-ness and hated wickedness therefore, God, your God, has set you above your compan-ions by anointing you with the oil of joy. (Amplified)

The verse in **Romans 12:1** says holy and well pleasing, holiness is not outward but it is an issue of the heart. People look at the outside but God looks on our hearts (**I Samuel 16:7**). I can remember coming into work every morning with a song and some of the officers would say I wish I could have some of what you have. But they did not want to submit to a holy life and die to self. They knew my joy was from Jesus. They did not know when I was going through tests and trials because the Lord strengthened me. He was my joy in the midst of my circumstances. He gave me grace that I still cannot comprehend. His ways are so much higher than our ways. His kingdom laws are opposite from what the world does. I thank Him and I love Him.

Engulfed in the glory of God's Son,
I thank Him for the souls He has won.
He died for us all, He draws us near,
The love of the Father, how precious and dear.

It will fill every corner, it will fill every place,
Engulfed in His presence and feeling His embrace.
I could never live without You, without Your love
    and Your Word.
Oh how I love You my King and my Lord.

You are the one that I adore.
Forever I will worship and sing to You my Lord.
You have captured my heart. I want to please You
    O God
I want to honor You and see Your love displayed
And proclaim Your goodness all the rest of my days.

I love to be in Your presence, a God I can feel,
You tear down walls and our hearts You heal.
My God how I love You, You have captured
    my heart.
I am addicted to Your love but that is not the
    only part.

So many sided is my God, I could never get enough.
There is always something new to open and explore.
Holy, righteous and awesome is the one that I adore.
Who could explain? Who can describe the majestic
    King of Kings,
The glorious Lord of Lords. I love You and I want
    to know You more.

You hear all my prayers not one is overlooked. I
    know You answer them.
I trust You more each day so patient and loving
    my King.
I will see Your glory and see You do great things.
With my heart I will praise You, with passion and
    all my strength.
You have got my attention and to show my love I
    will go to any length.
I want to learn of You, show me Your ways,
My loving wonderful Father, the Ancient of Days.

Holiness brings the anointing and the more anointed a person is, the more God requires holiness. His Word says to live by the Spirit and not by the flesh **(Romans 8)**. With the help and the grace of God we can crucify our flesh by the power of the Holy Spirit and through self-discipline and self-control. A person who has anointing without character is dangerous. I have seen this type of person. Living a holy life builds character. I want to be a vessel for God's anointing. I would never want to bring dishonor to His name. I want to have character before operating in the gifts of God. I want to be good to people and treat them well, do a good job, walk in excellence, and have a good attitude. I want to show people the love of Jesus not just say, "Jesus loves you." Character is developed and then total surrender and submission to God brings the power. When you are totally surrendered to God, you trust Him no matter what test, trial, or problem comes. You quote the Word like Jesus did to Satan while being tempted in the wilderness. We must remember what God says no matter what the circumstances, or situations look like, no matter what people say or what the outcome of the situation is.

I thank the Lord that He changes us from glory to glory. We all have issues in different areas whether it is smoking, drinking, pornography, overeating, complaining, gossiping, judging others, lying, stealing or whatever. But I want to be holy and please my Lord. I want God's presence in my everyday life in every area. Our body is the temple in which the Spirit of God dwells. We are a vessel that God uses to express the anointing.

I Peter 1:15-17 But as the One who called you is holy, you yourselves also be holy in all your conduct and manner of living. For it is written, you shall be holy, for I am holy. And

if you call upon Him as Father who judges each one impartially according to what he does, you should conduct yourselves with true reverence throughout the time of your temporary residence. (Amplified)

Ecclesiastes 9:8 Let your garment be white and let your head not lack oil. (KJV)

I Corinthians 3:16-17 Do you not discern and understand that you are God's temple and that God's Spirit has His permanent dwelling in you. If anyone does hurt to God's temple or corrupts it or destroys it, God will do hurt to him and bring him to the corruption of death and destroy him. For the temple of God is holy and that you are. (Amplified)

If we want God to use us, anoint us, work through us, release His power through us, we must humble ourselves, bring our flesh under subjection through self-denial, and separate ourselves from things that appear evil (**Thessalonians 5:22**). There is a price to pay for the anointing. We must die if we are really to live.

II Corinthians 4:11 For we who live are constantly being handed over to death for Jesus' sake, that the life of Jesus also may be evidenced through our flesh which is liable to death. (Amplified)

II Corinthians 6:17 So, come out from among and separate yourselves from them, says the Lord and touch not any unclean thing: then I will receive you kindly and treat you with favor. (Amplified)

I John 2:20 But you have been anointed by the Holy One, and you know all things. (Amplified)

The anointing brings revelation and God will release wisdom. Walking in God's anointing allows you to see things you cannot see in the natural mind, hear things you cannot hear in the natural, and sense things you cannot sense in the natural mind. When you see and hear things, God will bring confirmation through His Spirit and through His Word. **John 16:13** The Holy Spirit will lead you into all truth. **Acts 10:38** The anointing gives you strength, ability, and power. We must do what God says and not be concerned of what man thinks. We need to fear God, not man and their opinions. Are you willing to pay the price for the anointing and presence of the Father? What are you going to do with the anointing once he releases it?

John 14:12 I assure you, most solemnly I tell you, if anyone steadfastly believes in Me, he will himself be able to do the things that I do; and he will do even greater things than these, because I go to the Father. (Amplified)

CHAPTER EIGHT

The Fear of the Lord

Psalm 111:10 The fear of the Lord is the beginning of wisdom: a good understanding have all they that do His commandments: His praise undureth forever. (KJV)

The Lord would also deal with me about the fear of God being the beginning of wisdom. I studied this extensively. I love to study but most of my revelation has come from what God has revealed to someone else. Through studying other people's messages I learned that there is a difference between a spirit of fear which God did not give us, **(He gave us a spirit of power, of love and of a sound mind II Timothy 1:7)** and the fear of the Lord. I have found that according to the Word of God, holy fear is a key to unlocking the treasures of salvation, wisdom and knowledge.

Isaiah 33:5-6 The Lord is exalted, for He dwells on high; He will fill Zion with justice and righteousness. And there shall be stability in your times, an abundance of salvation, wisdom, and knowledge; the reverent fear and worship of the Lord is your treasure and His. (Amplified)

Psalm 34:9 O fear the Lord, you His saints! For there is no want to those who truly revere and worship Him in godly fear. (Amplified)

Proverbs 10:27 The fear of the Lord prolongeth days: but the years of the wicked shall be shortened. (KJV)

Romans 1:20-21 For every since the creation of the world, His invisible nature and attributes, that is, His eternal power and divinity, has been made intelligible and clearly discernable in and through the things that have been made. So men are without excuse. Because when they knew and recognized Him as God, they did not honor and glorify Him as God or give Him thanks. But instead they became futile and godless in their thinking and their senseless minds were darkened. (Amplified)

I heard someone preach that we serve the Lord in the image we have created of Him, and by our own standards and not by who He truly is. I have heard people in the church say God is my friend so I can say anything to Him, He understands my heart. They say that because they want to constantly complain even to God. Or well my heart is right, when they are doing something wrong. It is true God understands our hearts better than we do. But people sometimes say things like that to justify their actions that are wrong and that contradict the Word of God. The fact is we are sometimes disobedient to the Word. God test us so *we* might see what is in our own hearts, He already knows what is there. If we have not puri-fied our hearts and cleansed our hands, we will not be able to pass God's test. He is good though, He will give us the same test again. I do not want to go around the same mountain like the Israelites did for forty years in the desert. Many of us do not pass the test because we desire comfort over obedience to God's will. We make Jesus our Savior but we need to give God complete lordship over our lives.

In **Exodus 21**, the Israelites complained and God sent fiery serpents to the people and the serpents bit them and a lot of Israelites died. In **Number 14:29** The Lord told the Israelites they would die in the wilderness because they murmured against Him. **I Corinthians 10:9-10** Says, we should not tempt the Lord as some did and were killed by the fiery serpents. Nor should we complain as some did and died. I believe we can pour out our hearts to God but a person who is not thankful will complain. We are carnal Christians, not perceiving the ways of God, if we are constantly going to Him with our everyday problems. He knows everything we have need of, if we would only trust Him and praise Him. We have so much to be thankful for and the Word **(Psalm 100:4)** says, we should enter into His gates with thanksgiving and into His courts with praise.

The only people in the scriptures that God called friends were the ones that trembled at His Word and His presence and were quick to obey. Where is our reverence and fear of the Lord? Are there any who tremble at His Word? I desire to be a friend of God and to be immediately and habitually obedient to Him. I think sometimes we become so familiar with God's presence and His grace that we treat what God says is holy and sacred as if it were common. I have taken God for granted. I would answer the phone right in the middle of God speaking to me and grieve the Holy Spirit. Like what could be more important than what the creator of the universe had to say? I repented and felt like such a jerk for taking Him for granted and being rude. But the presence of God had lifted. I just knelt down and cried because I had let that precious moment pass and I could not get it back. The Holy Spirit is sensitive. It is almost like when I would get offended by my ex-husband. He would get angry at work or while he was shooting pool. He would come home yelling or cursing about the situation. He would be so angry sometimes and I would just be quiet. I would not leave but I would just sit quietly. I waited until he finished venting. It would be a little while before I felt comfortable talking freely. I did not want to upset him any further. I would sometimes go in another room and read my Bible or pray.

Also, when my ex-husband would watch secular television that portrayed situations contrary to God's Word. I would go in the other room. I think the Holy Spirit feels the same way. We are the temple of the living God. The Holy Spirit must feel so uncomfortable when we are sinning. I believe He is offended by our actions that do not line up with the will of God and the Word of God.

II Corinthians 6:16 What agreement can there be between the temple of God and idols? For we are the temple of the living God; even as God said, I will dwell in and with and among them and will walk in and with and among them, and I will be their God and they shall be my people. (Amplified)

Under the old covenant God's presence dwelt in the tabernacle, then the temple of Solomon but now God dwells in the temple found in the hearts of His sons and His daughters. We must count the cost for following Christ. It cost everything. A disciple lays down his life completely for the Master. A lot of people love God but they do not fear Him. We must make Him Lord of our lives. Converts may desire the benefits and the blessings of God but they often do not have the endurance to last through the testing and trials until the end. They do not want to die to self and live the life of a disciple. I pray, "Father please help us and give us the strength to endure and remain steadfast until the end." The love of God must be coupled with the fear of the Lord. I heard someone say, "What limits our love for God is the lack of holy fear." I do not want my love for Him to be limited. I want to know Him in all of His glory. If we want the continual presence of God, we must have a holy fear. Sin seems rampant in the church among members and leaders. The Word states, the judgment of God begins in the house of God (**I Peter 4:17**).

Psalm 25:14 The secret of the Lord have they who fear Him, and He will show them His covenant and reveal to them its meaning. (Amplified)

Psalm 115:11 You that fear the Lord, trust in the Lord: He is their help and their shield. (Amplified)

Ecclesiastes 8:11-12 Because the sentence against an evil work is not executed speedily, the hearts of the sons of men are fully set to do evil. Though a sinner does evil a hundred times and his days are prolonged, yet surely I know that it will be well with those who fear God, who revere and worship Him, realizing His continual presence. (Amplified)

Romans 11:22 Then note and appreciate the gracious kindness and the severity of God: severity toward those who have fallen, but God's gracious kindness to you,

provided you continue in His grace and abide in His kindness; otherwise you will be cut off. (Amplified)

There is a prison where dead souls lay,
They want their freedom but cannot get away.
They made their choices that ended in death,
Their lives meant nothing and there's nothing left.
Nothing but stubble, hay and wood,
It was burned by fire and nothing stood.

The test of time cannot erase,
The choices made, their own mistakes.
Life is full of questions and test it is true,
But you can have answers it is up to you.
Do you seek diligently? Do you knock?
Do you want truth or will you just mock?

God is calling for outlaws, those willing to run
    the race,
To see His kingdom come, who will not hide
    their face.
They will face any danger and not back down,
They will do it for the glory of the King and
    for their crown.

A new breed is coming out and is already here.
What is it you love? What do you fear?

How near is Jesus? Do you know His heart?
Do you feel His passion? Are you doing your part?

People may have an anointing from God on their lives but be far from God. The spiritual gifts can still operate in those people that are not pleasing to the Lord. We must love and fear God above all else. When we fear God, we put His interest and desires above our own. I want a deeper revelation of the heart of God and of the fear of the Lord. God has a remnant of people who love and fear Him. He will fill this remnant with His glory just like on the day of Pentecost.

Proverbs 22:11 He who loves purity and the pure in heart and who is gracious in speech, because of the grace of his lips will he have the king for his friend. (Amplified)

Psalm 55:19 God will hear and humble them, even He who abides of old-Selah- because in them there has been no change, and they do not fear, revere, or worship God. (Amplified)

I think about David in **I Chronicles 21**. David told Joab to number the people. Joab asked David why he would do this and bring guilt upon Israel. David wanted it done anyway. It says that the king's order was detestable to Joab. God was displeased because of this and He smote Israel. David then realized he had sinned against God and prayed. God sent a pestilence and 70,000 men of Israel were slain. In verse 16, David saw the angel of the Lord standing between earth and the heavens with his sword drawn and outstretched over Jerusalem. David and the elders fell on their faces and David repented to the Lord. David was told by a seer called Gad to build an altar to the Lord. King David again said he would not offer anything to the Lord that cost him nothing. David offered burnt offerings and peace offerings and called upon the Lord. Then the Lord commanded the angel to put the sword back into the sheath.

Hebrews 10:31 It is a fearful (formidable and terrible) thing to incur the divine penalty and be cast into the hands of the living God. (Amplified)

In **Acts 5:1-11**, we see that Ananias and his wife Sapphira sold a piece of property they owned. They brought only a portion of the money to the apostles and kept back some of the money. The scriptures say that they not only lied to men but to God. Ananias and his wife fell dead and great terror and dread seized the people. The fear of the Lord must come back in the Body of Christ. He is a loving and wonderful God but He is also a God to be feared. God is a God of judgment. How long do we think we can go on walking in sin and depend on the mercy and the grace of God?

There are some who will escape judgment because
   they obeyed.
They accepted Jesus Christ and the price He already
   paid.

But look to the sky. Do you see Him coming? On a
   white horse He is drawing near.
The heavenly armies are following, the beast they
   do not fear.
His robe is dipped in blood, the blood of the saints.
He is coming with a vengeance. He will release the
   restraints.

He is coming with judgment. He is called Faithful
   and True.
He is come to carry out the Word of God just like
   He said He would do.
A sword proceeded from His mouth and the
   remnant they were slain.
They were thrown into the lake of fire. Not one of
   them remained.

(Revelation 19)

I want to love God and His truths more than my
own life. I pray the Lord judges me and corrects
me here on earth before I go to heaven. I want to
repent so I can serve Him more perfectly. I do not
want to deceive myself about sin in my life. I want
to see truth. I seek to love God and love His people.
I attempt to live in order to help and give to others,
not see what I can get from them. I believe true love
serves, gives to others and glorifies God. To know
the love of God and the truth of His Word but live a
life where you seek to please yourself, is something
we will answer for later.

I sometimes get irritated with people and reject them. I am really rejecting God because His Word says that the least you do unto your brethren you do unto Him. In my arrogance, pride and rebellion, I thought the world revolved around me. As a police officer, I have brushed people off as if there issue were not important enough for my time because they did not understand the law. Instead of taking time to explain it and hear them out, I would treat their problem as if it were not a big deal. I am sure I made some of them feel inferior. Here I am a Bible toting Christian, but no fear of the Lord. God did not reject me because of all of my daily failures. He walks in love and even covers me when I am wrong and do not deserve it. He went to the cross for our sin and our failures. There were times when God would give me revelation about a person or situation. He would then show someone else maybe a couple of months later. I would have an attitude of, "Well God showed me that months ago". I was making myself greater by making them feel less than. I so want the grace to walk in love and humility before man and God. I am eager to live what I preach. I do not want to promote myself and prove myself to others. I want to exalt the Lord and not Grace McLeod. I seek to walk in pure love and let everything I do be worship unto the Lord. One day we will face the judgment seat of Christ. We will have to answer for the things we do here on earth.

Philippians 2:3 Do nothing from factional motives [through contentiousness, strife,

selfishness, or for unworthy ends] or prompted by conceit or empty arrogance. Instead, in the true spirit of humility (lowliness of mind) let each regard others as better than and superior to himself [thinking more highly of one another than you do yourself]. Amplified

CHAPTER NINE

Walking in Love

Having said all of this though, the Lord is teaching me to love others. I have such a long way to go. I do not want to continue to have to take the same test over and over. I want to pass them the first time. I have found that love can melt the hardest of hearts. When I first became a police officer there were not many women working for the agency where I was employed. As a matter of fact, they did not like women and did not think they should be in law enforcement. God has done an awesome work there since I was first employed. But when I first started it was very hard. Police officers see many situations that are not pleasing. We see a lot of deceased in various ways, natural death, shootings, automobile accidents, suicides, fires, etc. We are called to other people's problems all day. We are expected to resolve them peacefully while remaining professional and neutral. I can remember answering calls where a child was killed and then I would have to just go on to the next call. You had to suppress your emotions and your desire to go home and love on your child or spouse and thank God for them. So many officers' hearts were hardened by the continual pushing aside of their emotions in the performance of their duty. I would make a point to love on the officers no matter how they treated me. They would call me "Holy Roller" and other names. They would tell me to turn down my Christian music when I was in the Detective Bureau. I would go hug them and tell them I was so sorry for having my music to loud. I would bring them breakfast, make them cookies or buy them lunch. I would show them the love of God. I told them I loved them and so did Jesus. I was led by the Spirit though, not being offensive to them but knowing they were having a bad day and were in need of love. I saw God turn so many of them around. Some of the officers are now bringing Bibles to work, not ashamed of the Gospel. Some have retired. I remembered one in particular that I never saw even smile the first several years I worked there. I kept loving him and loving him. The last year before he retired, he would not only smile at me but would hug me. It was a huge break through for this man. I knew he never had anyone love him because he was cruel to people. I also knew it was because he had been hurt and he did not want to let anyone get close to him. I do not know if anyone ever showed him love before. I have had officers cry and pour out their hearts to me about different situations in their lives. They knew I would not tell anyone what they shared with me. I have been so blessed by God that He would use me in this way. I have such a long way to go in my love walk. I know God does not like everything I do, but He loves me no matter what. His love is not based on what I do. I do not have to earn His love; it is freely given. I want to walk in this unconditional love with others.

I Corinthians 13: 1-8 If I speak in the tongue of men and angels, but have not love, I am only a noisy gong or a clanging cymbal. And if I have prophetic powers, and understand all the secret truths and mysteries and possess all knowledge, and if I have faith, so that I could remove mountains, but have not love, I am nothing. Even if I dole out all that I have [to the poor in providing] food, and if I surrender my body to be burned, and have not love, I gain nothing. Love endures long, and is patient and kind; love never is envious nor boils over with jealousy, is not boastful or vainglorious, does not display itself haughtily. Is not conceited; is not rude and does not act unbecomingly. Love does not insist on its own rights or its own way, for it is not self-seeking; it is not touchy or fretful or resentful; it takes no account of the evil done to it. It does not rejoice at injustice and unrighteousness, but rejoices when right and truth prevail. Love bears up under anything and everything that comes,

is every ready to believe the best of every person, its hopes are fadeless under all circumstances, and it endures everything. Love never fails. As for prophecy it will be fulfilled and pass away; as for tongues they shall be destroyed and cease, as for knowledge, it shall pass away. (Amplified)

I John 4:8 He that loveth not knoweth not God; for God is love. (KJV)

I Peter 1:22 Since by your obedience to the Truth through the [Holy] Spirit you have purified your hearts for the sincere affection of the brethren, [see that you] love one another fervently from a pure heart. (Amplified)

I work down town Pensacola a lot on off duty assignments to earn extra money. I encounter all types of people. I usually work a theatre and I stand outside to see who comes by. The theatre is near several bars and a coffee shop where teenagers hang out. There are a lot of teenagers that are the "Gothic" type. I witness to them about the love of Jesus all the time. One of them told me recently that he had gone to church but no one hugged him like they did everyone else. He said no one even came and sat by him. I understand some people, like the retired officer I spoke of above; do not know what love is because they never had anyone love them. As Christians we must walk in love, grow in love, and practice loving others. Words are easy to say but what do our actions say. Recently, I worked a Christian talent show at the theatre. I was praying for a child who bumped into a wall and had a big knot on her head. A Christian lady from the program said to me, "You really need to pay attention to what is going on outside." I asked why what is more important than this hurt child. She said, "One of those people dressed in all black is just standing outside the door looking in and something needs to be done." These kids usually had chains hanging from their waist. They had all different colors of hair, sometimes spiked straight up. They would often have black lipstick on, black fingernail polish and sometimes black teardrops coming from their eyes. I believe the chains are symbolic of the bondage they live in. And the tears are for the loneliness and rejection they feel. I told the lady that it was probably one of the kids looking for me because I always hugged them and ministered to them. Her countenance changed. She said, "That is so awesome that you minister to those kids." I could tell from her initial response that she wanted me to tell them to leave. I just want to love them for who they are just like the Lord loves me. Actions require us to sacrifice and be kind to others even if they are not like us. I also see a lot of homeless in down town Pensacola while working at the theatre. Some of them are a product of a lot of wrong choices and some are mentally ill but we all need the love of Jesus no matter where we are in this walk of life. Jesus can come and turn around any situation no matter how hopeless it may seem to be. I attempt to be good to others, to find something good and encouraging to say not to find fault. We need to pay attention to the Lord and consult Him about what He wants us doing. He alone knows what people need. Sometimes He will have me bring a correcting word not a hug. I have to seek Him when I am making decisions in my life and for the lives of others. Love comes in many forms. Sometimes it is hugs and encouragement but sometimes it is through correction.

Hebrews 12:6 For the Lord corrects and disciplines everyone whom He loves, and He punishes, even scourges, every son whom He accepts and welcomes to His heart and cherishes. (Amplified)

II Timothy 3:16-17 All scripture is given by inspiration of God, and is profitable for doctrine, for reproof, for correction, for instruction in righteousness: that the man of God may be perfect, thoroughly furnished unto all good works. (KJV)

It is the love of God, not what man can give that will touch the hearts of people. I pray for the unconditional love of God to be manifested in my life. God's Word says, if you love Me you will obey Me. How else can we obey but by being sensitive to what the Holy Spirit has to say for each situation we encounter.

Ephesians 3:17-20 That Christ may dwell in your hearts by faith; that ye, being rooted and grounded in love, May be able to comprehend with all the saints what is the breadth, and length, and depth, and height; And to know the love of Christ, which passeth knowledge, that ye might be filled with all the fullness of God. Now unto Him that is able to do exceeding abundantly above all that we ask or think, according to the power that worketh in us. (KJV)

Soak in the presence of His Son,
And thank Him for the things He has done.
Be filled to overflowing with the love of God,
Anointing, anointed from heaven above.

Flowing from the throne of grace,
It will flow from here (His presence) to every place,
High in the mountains and over the hills,
It is the love of God that heals.

Over and over from place to place,
I will sing of His goodness. I will sing of His grace.
Like a river flowing freely I will pour out His plan,
From here in this place to foreign lands.

Oh how beautiful, the love of the Savior,
The kindness, the mercy, the love that endures
    forever.
Oh how awesome the love of the King,
He will use empty vessels to do great things.

The King of Kings, the Lord of Lords,
He is powerful and mighty to open all doors.
No one does He overlook from the greatest to the
    least,
We will all join together for the heavenly feast.

Like sheep we will follow, like lambs we will obey
The voice of the Father forever and today.

Our purpose in life is for God's pleasure, His purpose, His honor and His glory. Our purpose is to complete the work He has called us to do. I want to live for God's glory. Once we decide to live for His glory, our circumstances and situations just do not make a whole lot of difference. Many of God's people are not progressing or developing the call of God on their lives because we want to be happy. Only God can make us and keep us truly happy. We must set ourselves in God's direction. And we must do what He has called us to do with excellence and integrity. We must be that empty vessel, empty of self and willing to lay down our lives to serve others. We must serve with a pure heart and pure motives and give God the glory.

CHAPTER TEN

Building Faith

I have found that doing things God's way is not always easy. We must step out in faith not knowing positively that we are in God's will. We believe we have a dream or Word from the Lord but it takes faith to obey and step out. God has blessed me so much in the last few years. I am beginning my new book titled <u>Showers of Blessings</u>. In this I will reveal how by the grace of God, I stepped out in faith in several areas of my life that brought unbelievable blessings. God is so faithful. I have such a long way to go and have learned so much about myself through this process. The flesh is strong and just when you think you have accomplished great leaps for the Lord; God will show you the truth about yourself. Then there will be another area that we must submit to Him. All I can say is that it is all worth it. He is worth it. Even if He had not blessed me as outrageously as He has, it would still be worth it. The maturing process is slow and steady. There is no short cut in the process. The caterpillar must stay in the cocoon for a certain number of days or the wings and body of the butterfly will not form properly. The full transformation will not take place. Therefore, the butterfly will be deformed and unable to fly. In Malachi 3, the Word says God sits as a refiner's fire over us. He watches over us while we are put through the fire, tests and trials of life. When He feels we are ready He will release us to accomplish great things and to build His kingdom.

The Lord asks me why I worry and doubt when He has told me to do something. He said that He always turns it out for my good. I am always glad I followed His promptings once I see the fruit. I usually thank the Lord that He helped me be obedient. It is always worth it even when it is a hard thing to do. Why do we worry and doubt? God will continue to build our faith and stretch us. Each year I can look back and see growth in my spiritual life. I am so thankful for that. God continues to increase us as we continue to grow in Him. He is so wonderful. I am now starting to spread my wings a little. I pray I will follow Him more quickly. I pray we will all learn to flow in the anointing and presence of God. I am excited about the things God is doing in these days. What a wonderful time to live and serve the Lord. Be blessed in Jesus mighty name.

For more information, testimonies or questions
contact Grace McLeod:

Grace McLeod Ministries
P.O. Box 3121
Morganton, North Carolina 28680
BHG Ministries@aol.com

Other books available:

Showers of Blessings

Psalms and Songs of His Handmaiden

Printed in the United States
135957LV00001B/4/A

9 781600 342196